Working with
Handplanes

Working with
Handplanes

The Editors of
Fine Woodworking

The Taunton Press

The Taunton Press
Inspiration for hands-on living®

The Taunton Press, Inc., 63 South Main Street, PO Box 5506, Newtown, CT 06470-5506
e-mail: tp@taunton.com

Jacket/Cover design: Susan Fazekas
Interior design: Susan Fazekas
Layout: Susan Lampe-Wilson
Front Cover Photographer: Michael Pekovich, courtesy *Fine Woodworking*
Back Cover Photographers: (left) Boyd Hagen, courtesy *Fine Woodworking;*
(top right) William Duckworth, courtesy *Fine Woodworking;* (bottom right)
Asa Christiana, courtesy *Fine Woodworking*

Library of Congress Cataloging-in-Publication Data
Working with handplanes : the new best of fine woodworking / The Editors
of Fine Woodworking.
    p. cm.
 ISBN 1-56158-748-6
 1. Planes (Hand tools) 2. Woodwork. I. Fine woodworking.
 TT186.W675 2005
 684'.082--dc22

                         2004016081
Printed in the United States of America
10 9 8 7 6 5 4 3 2 1

The following manufacturers/names appearing in *Working with Handplanes* are trademarks:
Bailey®, Bedrock®, Bridge City Tool Works®, Carborundum®, Dapra®,
Dremel®, Dykem®, Greenfield Tool®, Kmart®, Kunz®, Lie-Nielsen®,
Lie-Neilsen Toolworks®, MacBeath HardwoodSM, Millers Falls®, Reid Tool
Supply Company®, Sandvik®, Stanley®, Starrett®, Woodcraft®

Working wood is inherently dangerous. Using hand or power tools improperly or ignoring
safety practices can lead to permanent injury or even death. Don't try to perform operations
you learn about here (or elsewhere) unless you're certain they are safe for you. If something
about an operation doesn't feel right, don't do it. Look for another way. We want you to
enjoy the craft, so please keep safety foremost in your mind whenever you're in the shop.

Acknowledgments

Special thanks to the authors, editors, art directors, copy editors, and other staff members of *Fine Woodworking* who contributed to the development of the articles in this book.

Contents

Introduction

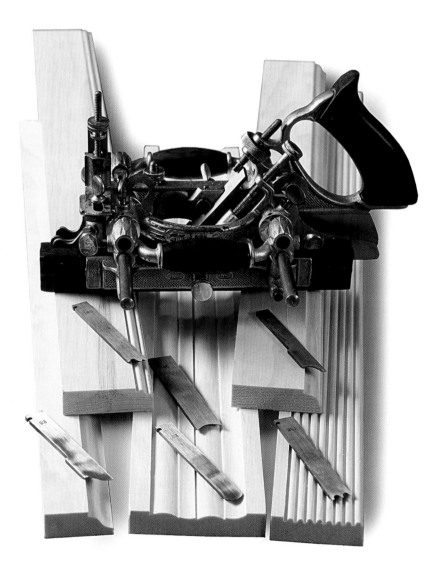

My first handplane almost ended my interest in woodworking. To say it was useless is an understatement. It did not plane. It hacked. I wasn't sure whether to fault the tool or the user.

I replaced the handplane with a belt sander, which performed well straight out of the box and saved my interest in woodworking. Although my skills were still primitive, the sander allowed me to complete some projects and they did not look hand hewn.

A few years later, the notion of hand-planing wood resurfaced. Determined to succeed, I took a class that devoted the first several sessions to simply flattening and sharpening the plane iron. Hours and hours of labor later, my hands stained black from fine steel and abrasive particles, I was rewarded with a shockingly sharp iron—so sharp, in fact, that it effortlessly shaved the hair on the back of my hand.

After I performed countless other tweaks to the body of the plane, I put it to wood. It performed well, slicing wood with a satisfying whish. The time spent on the tune-up was well worth it.

Woodworkers have many choices today when it comes to handplanes. The finest ones work well right out of the box. But all require maintenance eventually. Whether you have some older, lesser quality tools in need of a tune-up or simply want to get the most out of quality handplanes, the articles in this book, taken from the pages of *Fine Woodworking* magazine, will ensure your success. Soon you will realize why handplanes are among the most pleasing of all woodworking tools to use.

—Anatole Burkin, editor of
Fine Woodworking

Making Music with a Plane

BY JAMES KRENOV

When I was in school in Sweden, we had regular European planes that had to be held in a certain way. For some reason, curiosity or whatever, I made a little wooden plane out of maple. Suddenly, my friends are gathered around, and we're making shavings. I real- ized the versatility of that little block of wood. It was comfortable with two hands on it. It was comfortable with one hand doing a tiny little edge or corner. It had a new dimension because it did not force me to relate to it very rigidly in one certain way.

I don't think that you can prove in a court of law that these little wooden planes make thinner or better shavings than any other plane. I think the emotional element is the main difference, not necessarily performance only. It's a connection, an intimacy. The really good plane becomes an instrument. It becomes something that you want to make music with.

I used to make planes as a kind of therapy. Between jobs, I couldn't be idle and sit around. I'd finish a piece and have time to catch my breath, so I'd make a couple of planes. Some I'd give away: I've never sold one, and I never will.

There's no magic in any tool until you put the magic in it. The magic doesn't come with the tool. There's no one plane that will do everything. Mine go from jointer size down to very small. My favorite one is the little cocobolo one pictured in *A Cabinetmaker's Notebook*. It was my favorite, and I gave it away to someone very nice. I don't have a sentimental attachment to the planes anymore. I just want the ones I have to work well for me, and it doesn't matter which one it is; they are all good.

Don't Be a Slave to Accuracy

You come to a point where you can either engineer a plane or follow your common sense logic and feelings about it and arrive at about the same point. I make a good plane and then somebody else comes along and tells me it's a good plane because this angle is like this, and this thing is like that, and you've got the wedge this way, and you've got the opening like that. And I say, "Oh, is that what makes it good? I didn't worry about that. I just made it."

So somewhere the engineer and the peasant reach a parting of the ways, which is true throughout the craft. You can get so exact that you immobilize yourself with accuracy. I joke about it. You buy this square, and you pay $400 for it and it's accurate to a 10,000th of an inch. Then

all you've got to do is get yourself a job with Boeing building 747s and it's great. It's what you want, but it's not a woodworker's measurement, and it never will be. Somewhere there is a flexibility that relates to the kind of person you are and the kind of work you do, and it has nothing to do with sloppiness. It's just flexible enough to keep you from being paralyzed.

Can you get results that are good with a metal plane? I think so, yes, and I've seen it. We've never said to our students here, "Put that thing away." As long as it's working well for them, and it's tuned up properly, and it's kept in perfect shape, and they do beautiful work. I would never want anyone to quote Jim Krenov as saying that you have to have a wooden plane. It's nice if you like them, but there isn't only one way.

Making Your First Plane a Success

My first suggestion would be to ask yourself, "Am I doing this out of curiosity, or do I believe in it? Do I intend to arrive at the point where this becomes the thing for me, and I know I can make a good wooden plane anytime I want to and I can do fine things with it?" If it's mere curiosity, then it becomes just like anything else we do for the sake of exercise. Just to prove that we can go through the ABCs of it.

I think it's important not to fail completely with the first plane, because then you might not make a second one. You could be missing something. Do try to get the essentials right on the first one, and get it to where, yes, it does work, and yes, I can make one better, and yes, I will make one better.

One key element is what happens when you raise or lower the pin in relation to where the shavings need to exit. You can put the pin so far down that you choke the plane up. But once you have this and a few other things right, then you're off and running. If I had the wood and the iron and

The first little attempt with a plane that succeeded may have been the turning point of my life.

the breaker, I'd have a plane done by evening, and I'd start using it the next morning. Tune it up, and forget about it.

The first little attempt with a plane that succeeded may have been the turning point of my life because it opened up the fact that tools can be better, that tools can be more personal and intimate. Had I failed, I might have just fallen back into the general pattern. That doesn't mean I wouldn't have become a cabinetmaker, but I might never have been able to make music as I try to do.

Don't Let Sharpening Take Over

A plane is no better than its cutting edge. But you can develop an imbalance in the relationship of your work and the sharpening. There should be a nice balance between the time you work and the time you care for your tools, whether it's a chisel, a knife, a plane or anything else.

The tendency ever since the Japanese waterstone thing is that people are more worried about the stone not being perfectly flat than about how they hold the iron or about working harmoniously. Even with a perfectly flat stone, they're not going to get what's needed. It's not in the stone. I observed in Japan some house builders who were pretty casual about their stones, yet they got their planes to sing.

There should be a balance there somewhere. Gradually, you arrive at a point where the sharpening is minimal rather than maximal. It won't be a chore anymore. You'll do it and do it fairly quickly.

I think that having two or three nice oilstones and a little bottle of kerosene can compete with having a Japanese waterstone, because the Japanese method of sharpening tools is almost an art form or ritual. Doing it haphazardly or not completing the process is neither here nor there. You can spend an awfully long time sharpening but what you're really doing is honing too much. If you hollow grind a tool, a very slight hollow, then all you need is to just hone until you get a tiny little burr, and then quickly move to a finer stone and not keep going on until you flatten out the hollow, because you'll always have the burr as long as you use that stone. So with just a few strokes, you get the scratches from the wheel off, and then you go to a finer stone right away.

I've had the same oilstones for 30 years, and I've never trued them up or anything, which doesn't speak well for me. I've got an old Carborundum that I found in Stockholm, a soft Arkansas and a hard Arkansas and a little kerosene and that's it. People wonder if I ever sharpen my tools because they hardly ever see me doing it. When I do, it's just a little bit. It becomes self-defeating if carried too far because you're fussing more about your tools than you are working, and at some point, fussing just takes over.

I've got planes I haven't touched or adjusted or sanded or trued up for several years. I just pick them up, and they're ready to go. One thing that is amusing is if the last time I set a plane the air was very dry and since then it has rained and increased in humidity, I'll pick up the plane and it won't cut because the wood has expanded a little bit and the iron is no longer protruding. The opposite is also true. If I set it on a very humid day or part of the year and later we get a cold snap, I'll pick it up and it will really dig in, cutting much too deeply. It's like a musical instrument that you have to tune up a little bit before you start the concert.

I look at the plane from behind rather than in front. I look at the bevel and lower my eye to the level of the plane itself. I can see the glint before the iron reaches the level of the bottom of the plane, and then I tap on the iron very lightly. You'll never get a good cut if the iron is not absolutely parallel with the bottom of the plane. You'll get an angled cut. You want to tap the iron itself, not the plane body. When you tap the plane body, you have no guarantee that the iron won't slip sideways as it moves forward or back. You do tap the back of the plane body to retract the iron. But readjust it by tapping the iron itself.

The wedge should not be too tight. You should be able to remove it easily with your fingers by just zig-zagging it out. The tendency is to really bear down on it, but you don't need to do that. You want a low-angle wedge. If you have a high-angle wedge, it's apt to kick out when you are doing coarse work.

You very seldom have to go back and true up a plane. If you notice a consistent misbehavior or if the plane tends to produce an arch or a dip, then you can fine-tune it. But it also becomes second nature with you. Where to press, how to do that. It's very minimal and elementary.

For Cabinetmaking, the Plane Is a Basic Tool

A plane is a favorite of mine by necessity. In other words, it is the tool in casework. With the kind of work that I and other cabinetmakers do most, it's almost indispensable. Because I started out not being able to afford a jointer and I only had a bandsaw, I discovered I couldn't even bandsaw anything without having a plane to true it up a little bit. I almost killed myself doing it, but it showed me how necessary the plane was, not how refined it should be but just how necessary it was.

I think there's a line between sentiment and positive emotion or creative emotion. In other words, you buy a yard sale tool and you fix it up as best you can and you know it will never sing, but it has something and gives you something emotionally. It has a sentimental value. Then there's this other element that is not sentimental, but is emotional, where you believe that you work better with this finely tuned instrument than you do with something more awkward or more coarse. That, I think, is the difference. You don't get carried away by the fact that it is an antique or that George Washington used it or something. You just think of what it will do and what you can do with it.

JAMES KRENOV works and teaches at the College of the Redwoods in Fort Bragg, Calif., and he has authored four books about craftsmanship and cabinetmaking. This article is adapted from conversations recorded in Fort Bragg in July 1996.

Straight Talk About Planes

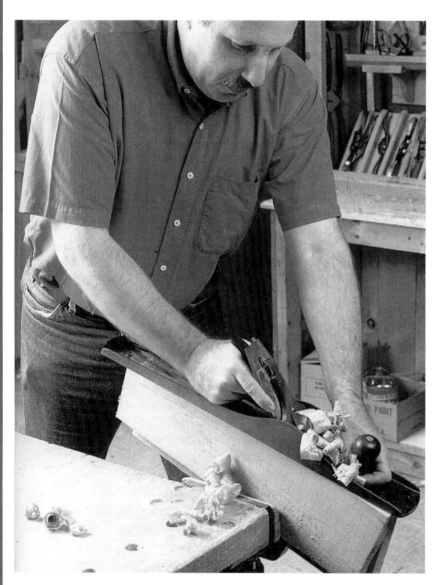

STRAIGHTENING A PAIR OF MATING EDGES with a jointer plane. To prepare boards for edge-to-edge glue-up, Starr matches up their face grain and folds them over. Then he evens up the edges and clamps the pair in his bench vise, so he can plane slightly downhill. Any error cancels itself when the edges are butted.

BY RICHARD STARR

Handplanes are essential wood-working tools. They've been found in just about every shop for the last 2,000 years. Even in modern shops with plenty of power machines, handplanes have an important place. Why? Because with a plane, you can chamfer or round a corner, trim a door edge, or true up a twisted board. You can clean the sawmill fuzz off a rough plank, leaving a smooth surface that's nearly sinful to caress. While you're at it, you can straighten a pair of board edges, so they'll butt together for a perfect glue joint (see the photo at left). You can even use a plane on a lathe to smooth a long tapered shape, like a baseball bat.

Just as every planing situation is unique, each woodworker uses and chooses planes differently. One person says to turn the adjuster this way, another says to turn it that way. I know a wonderful woodworker who uses his massive jointer plane on short sections of end grain, which is a tricky job commonly assigned to a miter or block plane. He says that he likes the heft and solidity of a large plane for this delicate work. He's right, of course—for him. That's

what is neat about these tools; everyone has his or her ideas about handplanes.

I'll pass along a few bench-plane and block-plane tricks I've picked up while teaching woodshop to kids over the past 21 years. Does this mean that what I'm going to tell you is the final word? Heck no. But, hopefully, it will help you sort through the variety of planes that are out there, so you'll see what works best for you in your situation. And maybe it will encourage you to tune and try planes in new ways.

How to Determine which Plane to Use for What

Bench planes are usually identified by the numbers given them by the Stanley company over a century ago (see the photo above). The biggest standard metal plane (Stanley No. 8) is 24 in. long, and the smallest in common use is a No. 3, which is 8 in. or 9 in. long, depending on which company made it. Aside from appearance, the biggest difference between planes is the kind of shaving each is set up to cut. Of course, there is overlap: By virtue of their adjuster mechanisms, modern metal planes are versatile enough to do different tasks. However, making drastic shaving alterations takes

time and may even require irreversible modification to the tool, such as filing the throat wider (for more on this, see the sidebar on pp. 12–13). Despite the possibilities, you can't expect a plane that's been set for fine work to hog off thick shavings, nor can a plane designed for scrub work be made to leave a shining, flat surface. So for starting out, it's wise to select a plane based on its length.

Sole length A plane's major function is to make things flat and/or square by cutting down high areas. By bridging over low spots and shallow undulations in a board, long planes can true up a board's face or edge easier and more accurately than shorter planes. This is true, provided the plane's sole is flat, of course.

In my shop, I keep a 24-in.-long jointer plane that's set to take a fine shaving in difficult wood. However, this doesn't necessarily mean that every time I need to flatten a board, I grab that 24-in. plane. If I'm working on a board that's only 18 in. square, or an edge that's a foot long, that huge plane is overkill. For stock in this range, I use a plane that's easier to handle—an 18-in.-long No. 6, traditionally called a fore plane.

Getting the Best Cut

Getting the best cut from your handplane is a matter of adjusting blade angle. For straight-grained woods, pushing your plane askew (right) lowers the angle of cut. To prevent tearout in figured woods, try grinding a top bevel on the blade (see the upper detail), so your plane acts like a scraper. Both standard- and low-angle block planes have their blades bevel up (see the lower detail).

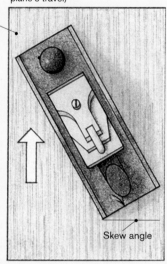

Normal effective angle
(Cutting angle parallel
to sole length)

Lowered effective angle
(Cutting angle parallel to
plane's travel)

Workpiece

Direction
of travel

Skew angle

Plane is hard to push
on difficult wood.

A skewed plane is easier to
push, but shaving is narrower.
Vary skew angle to find optimum effort and surface.

Detail: Bench-plane edge

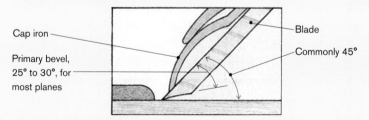

Cap iron

Primary bevel,
25° to 30°, for
most planes

Blade

Commonly 45°

Detail: Block-plane edge

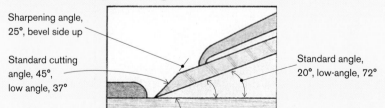

Sharpening angle,
25°, bevel side up

Standard cutting
angle, 45°,
low angle, 37°

Standard angle,
20°, low-angle, 72°

In my woodshop class, we call the No. 6 a finishing plane because it's often the last one we surface the face of a board with.

Blade width What about the width of cut? Blades can vary in width from 1⅜ in. for a block plane to 2⅝ in. for a jointer. Longer planes generally have wider blades. An exception to this rule is the wide-body planes that have a ½ appended to their number designation. For instance, Record currently produces a No. 5½, which is 14 in. long and has a 2⅜-in.-wide blade (compared to 2 in. for a regular No. 5). If you shop for used tools, you'll occasionally come across others, like Stanley's 4½ and 6½ models. You may even find a 5¼ body, which has a 1¾-in.-wide blade. One advantage of a wider blade is it takes a broader shaving and covers a board faster. A more subtle advantage occurs at the blade's edge.

Slightly Crowned Blades Cut Better

Many cabinetmakers grind a plane blade with a very slight crown or curve at the edge. A crowned blade takes a shallower cut toward its sides. A plane with a straight edge can leave obvious tracks on the board's face due to the square corners of the blade. With a properly crowned blade, you can produce a shaving whose edges feather to zero thickness. A crowned blade's tapered cut leaves a slightly rippled surface with no obvious tracks. The amount of crown must be minimal (we're talking paper thicknesses here) or else you'll wind up with a surface that's too wavy. That's why wider blades are a plus; they allow the crown to be flatter, yielding a shaving the same thickness as a narrower blade but with much less tell-tale overlap.

In addition, the wood fibers at the edges of a crowned blade's shaving are cut from the surface rather than being torn away. Imagine using a chisel to plow a groove across the grain of a board. The tool is hard to push, and you tear out wood left and right. Now do the same job with a gouge, which, because of its U-shape, severs wood along the sides of the cut. The groove is clean, and the tool pushes easily. Similarly, it's easier to push a plane with a crowned blade. This is true even if you set it deeper to remove the same volume of wood as a straight-edge plane. The best example of this principle is a scrub plane, which has a narrow, highly crowned blade that removes stock quickly. Scrub or hogging planes work best diagonally or at right angles to the grain, where rising or falling wood fibers are of no consequence. The resulting wavy surface is easy to clean up with a fine-set smooth plane.

Blade Angles: Different Cuts for Different Woods

Nearly all bench-plane blades form a 45° angle with the wood. For most work, this is ideal. But, there are other considerations, both in theory and practice. In his book, *Understanding Wood*, (The Taunton Press) Bruce Hoadley explains what effect a plane's blade angle has on wood at the microscopic level. The Victorian expert Charles Holtzapffel in volume II of *Turning and Mechanical Manipulation* (reprinted by Early American Industries Assoc., Levittown, N.Y.), suggests various (iron) pitches for woods of increasing hardness. He names them as follows: 45° (common), 50° (York), 55° (middle), and 60° (half). Holtzapffel, always the pragmatist, goes on to say that really tough woods, like boxwood, may require a vertical blade or one that leans slightly forward to provide a scraping action.

Same tool, different slants Making a wooden plane lets you choose a cutting angle appropriate for a job. What surprises many people is that you can also select the angle of a metal plane.

PLANE SOLES VARY MOSTLY IN WIDTH AND LENGTH, **but there are other differences, too. From the bottom up: a wooden scrub plane with horn-beam sole, a No. 8 jointer plane with narrow throat, a No. 4 smooth plane, a No. 4 with corrugated sole and a low-angle block plane with adjustable throat.**

To increase the angle of cut, you can grind a top bevel on the blade. The price of a steep angle or of a cap iron set very close to the cutting edge (which accomplishes almost the same thing) is that the plane becomes harder to push. But reducing the blade angle makes planing easy and requires no tool modification at all. You simply push the plane askew. Normally, the effective angle of cut is parallel to the blade's length. If you measure the angle of the blade to the wood in line with a skewed plane's direction of travel (say 45°), you'll find that the effective angle is seriously reduced. The farther you turn the plane, the lower the cutting angle and the narrower the shaving. Shavings cut askew no longer curl up on themselves, but form spirals as though each strand of wood steps sideways to make room for the next. The same logic applies to both chisels and planes, regardless of whether they're cutting face, edge, or end grain.

Block planes A block plane's blade is installed upside down, or bevel up, which eliminates the angle problem. Standard block planes are usually 5 in. to 7 in. long and seat their blades at 20°. The low-angle variety (see the drawing on p. 10), which are great for planing end grain, have blades tilted at 12°. A block plane's actual cutting angle depends on how steep you grind the bevel. If the bevel is 25°, then adding a standard blade angle of 20° yields a bevel-to-wood, or cutting angle, of 45°. Honing a secondary (micro) bevel, usually 5° or so, at the tip of the primary bevel will increase the angle of cut.

When block-planing, always try skewing the tool 45° while holding it firmly with two hands. I like to keep a few block planes set up for different cuts. The more sophisticated block planes have adjustable throats. Lightweight and easily handled, these little friends are instantly ready for precision trimming, for quick-and-dirty jobs or for smoothing a wicked piece of wood.

Planing Made Easier

As a general rule, it's the blade's width, not its length, which makes a plane difficult to push. If you're sweating too hard, try a narrower plane. Another effort improver is to minimize the friction between the plane and your board. Planes with wooden soles slide quite well because they lightly burnish the work. Japanese planes go a step further. Their shaped soles touch a workpiece in four places only: at the front, ahead and aft of the blade, and at the rear. A few metal plane manufacturers have also tried to reduce surface contact. Take a plane with a corrugated sole (see the photo on p. 11), for example. Stanley claims the grooves prevent

Getting a Plane to Work the First Time

You've just bought a new handplane, and you're in a hurry to get it working properly. To set up a plane for general planing around the shop, here are the tune-up steps that I recommend:

1 Chamfer all around the plane's sole, as shown in the photo below. Factory edges and corners are often so sharp they'll leave marks on the wood.

2 Set the frog so it makes a continuous surface at the beveled back of the throat (see the bottom photo at right). Moving the frog forward of this position leaves the cutting end of the blade unsupported where it counts. A few of the better (older) planes have stepped frogs, which support the blade even when the throat is small.

3 Smooth the convex surface of the cap iron's chip breaker, and undercut the lead edge of the chip breaker so that it makes tight, uniform contact with the blade. Both of these jobs are easily done on a coarse diamond stone (see the top photo at right). Finally, make sure there is enough bend in the cap iron, so it will make tight contact at its front edge.

4 Flatten the back of the blade on the coarse diamond stone. Hone until the first half inch is gray, which indicates that there's complete contact with the stone. Next, surface the blade's back on a fine diamond or Carborundum stone. Use a similar procedure to sharpen the bevel (see the drawing on p. 10). Although entire articles have addressed sharpening, I get good results using the following method: Start on a coarse diamond stone, and

then go to a fine one before finishing up both sides of the edge on a hard Arkansas stone or water stone.

5 Assemble the cap iron and blade and tighten the screw. Check for light between the contact points of the two parts (see the lower photo at right). Any gap between chip breaker and blade, however small, will clog with shavings, and the plane will choke and stop cutting. Resurface the edges, if necessary, and set the front of the cap iron between $\frac{1}{32}$ in. and $\frac{1}{16}$ in. from the end of the blade.

6 Examine the leading edge of the lever cap. If the edge is blunt, dress it using a rocking motion on the diamond stone. Also, flatten the edge's bottom (see the photo below), so chips won't jam where the lever cap contacts the cap iron.

7 Put the plane together, and check the size of the throat. Because I always adjust the frog so it supports the blade best, the throat is always open to its maximum. Even so, I often find that the throat is too small and not always parallel to a properly set blade. The only fix is to file metal sparingly from the throat's leading edge (see the photo below).

When I buy a used handplane, I basically follow the same tune-up routine, although I pay more attention to the tool's condition initially. If the plane's throat doesn't need filing and if the sole is flat, I can get a plane ready to go in under an hour of careful work. The best thing about well-cared for old planes, like Stanley planes made around 1920, is that most of them have heavy bodies, good-fitting cap irons and lever caps, and blades that hold a nice cap.

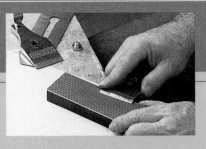

FLATTEN THE EDGE OF A CAP IRON using a sequence of coarse, medium, and fine diamond stones. Next flatten, or lap, the back of the plane's blade before honing its bevel. Then dress the edge of the lever cap.

LIGHT REVEALS GAPS. Cabinetmaker Mario Rodriguez slides the back of a blade along the mating edge of the cap iron to reveal where chips may clog. If no cracks of light appear, he sets the contact point $\frac{1}{16}$ in. or less from the end of the blade.

Getting a Bench Plane Up and Running

Fine-tuning makes for good shavings. A cross-sectional view of a plane shows where you should check and what you can adjust to get a smooth cut, whether the tool is new or used. The cutaway body of this jack plane illustrates the critical relationships between blade, cap iron, lever cap, frog, and sole.

Dress leading edge of lever cap if it's blunt of not straight.

Flatten and polish top (back) of blade, and then hone the bevel.

Set the frog so it continues the bevel at the plane's throat.

File or grind a chamfer all around the plane's sole.

With plane assembled, adjust size and check shape of throat (blade edge should be parallel with opening); carefully file front of throat if needed.

Check junction between the cap-iron edge and blade back; gaps allow shavings to choke the tool. If needed, refine contact points on diamond stone.

suction between the plane and the board, but I've never been convinced. Instead, I rub the sole of all my planes every few minutes with a paraffin block. I coat the area where the most friction (wear) occurs: at the section of the sole just ahead of the blade. Waxing or oiling other places on the sole doesn't seem to matter.

Of course, the best way to ease any handplaning project is to select your stock carefully. Finding straight-grained lumber is worth the premium in time and dollars.

Flattening a Plane Sole by Hand

To many woodworkers' surprise, the sole of an antique plane or even a new plane can need flattening. Even if the sole is flat when you buy the tool, heavy planing eventually wears a sole out of true. When this happens, you don't have to send your plane to a machine shop or spend tedious hours passing your plane over stones.

The flattening method I use still relies on an abrasive surface for the final step, but I begin with more aggressive means to speed the job along. The technique also works on flattening backs of chisels and plane blades. I learned the procedure from a master machinist friend, Eric Mingrino, who

recommends first flattening the sole of a block plane. Later, you can work your way up to wider, longer plane bottoms.

Check if the sole is out of flat: To determine whether a plane sole is out of true, first apply a film of DYKEM Hi-Spot, a non-drying blue ink, over the entire sole. Using a precision straightedge, identify any high spots by dragging the straightedge across the sole, as shown in the left photo below.

Level high spots with a scraper: To quickly level high spots of the sole, I use a tool that may be unfamiliar to woodworkers: a 14-in.-long machinist's

scraper (also available from machinist-supply stores or from Dapra). Both old-style scrapers, which have brazed-on tips, and newer ones, which have indexed carbide-tips, have file-like wooden handles. Experimenting with various scraping angles yields cuts ranging from fine scratches to coarse swirls. You don't want to remove excess material, or you'll risk opening up the throat too much. I flex and push the scraper vigorously on needed areas only (see the middle photo below), and then I recheck the bottom. It's critical that the sole be dead flat ahead of the throat, where most of the wear occurs.

CHECK FOR FLATNESS. Machinist's bluing and a good straightedge allow Rodriguez to find high spots on the sole of this block plane. On bench planes, he retracts the blade, but doesn't remove it, so that the body of the plane stays stressed.

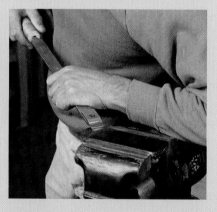

REDUCE HIGH AREAS (identified by a lack of ink) using a machinist's scraper. Scraper tips, which may be permanent or replaceable, like the carbide tip here, produce a fine graphite-like powder that accumulates on the sole.

SMOOTH THE PLANE'S BOTTOM with a mill file. Remaining high spots show up as dull gray. Once the ink disappears, draw-file the surface.

Finally, for the woods that demand special skills, experiment and develop. If you are working curly maple or a twisted chunk of hard exotic, for example, just be patient as you try various blade settings and planing motions.

RICHARD STARR, author of *Woodworking with Your Kids*, reprinted in 1990 by The Taunton Press, teaches middle school in Hanover, N. H.

Once the straightedge removes large patches of ink, it's time for filing.

Surface the whole sole with a file: Go over the entire sole with a 12-in.-long, flat, second-cut mill file. These large mill files are heavy and long enough to make the job easy, and they flatten the surface uniformly. Filing slightly askew, cleanly remove the last traces of bluing (see the right photo on the facing page).

At this point, the sole should be true. Now it needs to be polished. To remove file marks, draw the file's teeth toward you perpendicular to the sole's length (called draw filing). Because much of the file overhangs the plane, be sure to keep the contact area flat while maintaining even pressure.

Sand out scratches with abrasive paper: The next step is to pass the plane back and forth over emery paper spray-glued to a flat machined surface (I use my jointer's feed table), as shown below. If you're not sure whether your jointer or saw table is flat, overlay it with a piece of ½-in.-thick plate glass, which is perfectly true, then the paper. When the plane bottom has a uniform look and checks out flat with the straightedge, repeat with increasingly finer grits of wet/dry paper until the plane bottom has a bright, reflective finish.

REMOVE FILE SCRATCHES AND BURRS from the sole with emery paper adhered to a flat table (bottom right). Eliminate other imperfections with wet/dry abrasive paper.

Four Planes That Earn Their Keep

BY SVEN HANSON

After 20 years of mechanizing and jigifying my woodshop, I have to admit that the four planes shown in the photo below are still my most cost-effective tools. Not all by themselves, mind you. But they work as part of a complementary system that capitalizes on the efficiency of machinery and power tools to do the bulk work quickly and on the versatility of hand tools, especially planes, to do fine detail work. The four planes that I use regularly—smooth plane, jack plane, low-angle block plane and bullnose plane—also

happen to be my favorite tools to use, period.

The Stanley Co. refined the designs of their cast-iron planes back in the late 1800s. Stanley-style planes, which are now made by a number of manufacturers, still deliver the goods in 1995. Sure, they take some time to master, but so do power tools. You have to set up planes properly and maintain them (see the sidebar on pp. 20–21), but investing a little time here will raise your work to a higher level. Even better, planes are quiet and don't make any dust. The joy of using finely crafted handplanes,

HANDPLANES COMPLEMENT POWER TOOLS. Clockwise from left: a No. 4 for smoothing and flattening, a No. 5 for truing edges, a bullnose chisel plane for cleaning up rabbets and joinery, and a low-angle block plane for chamfering and trimming.

16

TWO VERSATILE WORKHORSES. The author uses a No. 4 smooth plane to flatten and smooth boards. With its sole waxed and skewed to the work, the plane easily removes mill marks from a piece of padauk. To joint edges, he uses the No. 5 jack plane in the background.

woodworkers' mainstays since Roman times, just puts the frosting on the cake.

Integrating Planes into Everyday Shop Work

For serious stock preparation, I use a table-saw, a bandsaw, a planer, a jointer, and several routers. Then I turn to my arsenal of planes. I'm not talking about antique, wooden planes here. These are modern, metal planes, carefully tuned to have flat soles with sharp, well-bedded blades set at the right depth of cut.

The Stanley Co. assigned numbers to their various planes. Bench planes started with a No. 1 (the smallest and least common) and ended with a No. 8 jointer plane, which is the largest. Numbers higher than eight just identify the type of plane and do not indicate size. In everyday shop work, I use a No. 4 smooth plane to level and smooth surfaces, a No. 5 jack plane to joint edges for glue-up and a No. 90 bullnose

plane to clean up rabbets and bevel inside corners.

I also use a low-angle block plane (Stanley No. 60½) as a utility player. It's great for one-handed jobs, like planing end grain, chamfering and truing. And it's great for getting into tight places. I like it for smoothing certain difficult woods, too. Here's the way I use each of the four planes in my normal work:

Use two smooth planes: one for flattening, one for smoothing I once tried to save six cents per board foot by buying unsurfaced boards and planing them to the right thickness with a scrub plane. After my arms turned to rubber and I was soaked in sweat, I decided to skip the scrub plane. It's much easier to buy surfaced lumber that's already fairly flat and smooth and consistent in dimension, color, and grain pattern.

I still use a plane to do a little hogging, though. Once in a while, I use my No. 4 Bailey (a high grade of Stanley) smooth

More than one authority on handplanes has said that the route to clean planing is paved by a thicker blade. After trying several of them, I have to agree. Even if a thick iron is poorly seated to the frog, the iron's greater thickness reduces vibration and, hence, the stuttering that you often get with a thin blade as it skips across the wood.

Thick blades used to be the norm. Some of the earliest ones were tapered in thickness over their length. Luckily, you can still get thick antique blades, which offer the advantage of laminated construction. Old blade forgers put a layer of very hard but brittle steel on the top of the blade over cheaper, softer, and more flexible steel. This yields a heavy blade that holds its edge for a long time.

Hock Handmade Knives offers new, thick replacement blades in a variety of sizes (available from Garrett Wade, 161 Avenue of the Americas, New York, NY 10013; 800-221-2942 or Frog Tool Co., 700 W. Jackson Blvd., Chicago, IL 60661; 800-648-1270). You can find thick antique blades at auctions, tool swaps, and flea markets.

But antique blades usually need work, such as removing rust pits, flattening the backs, and sharpening. Also, you may have to narrow the iron to fit a new plane body or extend the cap-iron screw slot. But boy, can these irons cut and last.

This, combined with the skew, makes for relatively easy work and minimal tearout.

I find smooth planes especially handy in two common situations. The first is where two pieces of wood intersect—as they do in a door frame. I plane the adjoining surfaces one at a time until they are flush. The other is when I'm taking down high spots to get an even surface. For both of these jobs, I use the finishing smooth plane, fitted with a blade set for a light cut. Because the frog is adjusted for a small throat, it supports the blade edge. Taking the time to make these adjustments makes the plane easy to push and produces a smooth finish. The drawings on p. 20 show what happens when the plane is adjusted correctly.

With the finishing smooth plane, I leave the cutting edge straight, but I round just the corners of the iron so they don't dig in. I skew the plane slightly and use shallow strokes in overlapping passes, which reduces tearout when I have to plane across or against the grain. I use slight pressure at the front of the sole during the start of a cut and shift pressure to the back as I finish. I do this to prevent rounding over the ends of the work. I'm actually lifting the heel and then the toe. To picture this, visualize the board from the side, and work as if you were planing a hollow in the middle by easing up on each end of the cut.

Regardless of which type of smooth plane I'm using, I hold the plane firmly without strangling it by the handles. Your hands can't feel what's happening if you use a death grip. Use a lighter grip, and let your fingers help guide the plane. To plane the edge of a board, wrap your fingers part way around the plane, and touch the sides of the wood. Use your fingers as a fence (see the photo on p. 17). To plane wide surfaces, rest your thumb on one side of the plane and fingers on the other. You can point your forefinger in the direction you're planing. If you aren't getting a good shaving, then expose less blade or sharpen it.

plane fitted with a thick, spare blade that has its edge rounded, like the tip of an adze. (See the sidebar above to learn more about thicker irons.) I grind and hone this plane iron at the usual 25° to 30° bevel, and by moving the frog and the iron, I adjust the throat (the opening formed by the edge of the blade in the mouth of the sole) so that it's fairly wide.

For general planing, however, I use two planes: a "roughing" smooth plane, which has the throat ⅛ in. open and the cap iron set back ¹⁄₁₆ in. from the edge of the blade, and a "finishing" smooth plane, which has a ¹⁄₁₆ in. or smaller throat and the cap iron set ¹⁄₆₄ in. or less back from the blade edge.

When making heavy cuts, like flattening a board, I skew the roughing plane to the grain to make a slicing cut. Because I slightly crown the edge of the blade in this plane, there's less contact with the wood.

A jack plane with a crowned blade is great for edge-jointing The jack plane, slightly longer than a smooth plane, probably got its name from either jack-of-all-trades or a mule. From either origin, you get the idea that this tool is a hard worker. Most furniture makers take a No. 7 or No. 8 plane to joint edges because they are long (over 20 in.) and heavy. I prefer a No. 5, 14-in.-long jack plane for this task. It takes more trial fitting of the boards, but the jack is easier to handle. You could even substitute a smooth plane for jointing, but it is a bit short. In any case, you'll need a blade profile suited to jointing, not smoothing.

The blade for jointing should be crowned so that the middle of the edge is about .01 in. higher than the corners. I've tried other shapes and found that an iron without a crown wanders like a car without a steering wheel.

There's another reason to crown the blade. To correct the edge of a board that's out of square with a straightedge blade, you have to choose between angling the blade to the sole or tilting the plane to cut down the high side of the edge.

It's hard to tilt the tool freehand such a small amount. Likewise, it's not easy to angle the blade in the plane accurately (I angle it the wrong way half the time). But if you use a crowned blade, you can correct a beveled edge by planing with one side of the iron on the high side of the board. With practice, you can straighten a twisted edge in a pass or two. Once you learn the right body English, you'll be getting joints that close as tightly as the doors to Scrooge's vault.

Other than having a crowned blade for jointing and a relatively open throat, I set the rest of my jack plane just like a finishing smooth plane. That is, the blade has a razor edge, the sole is flat and the frog is seated firmly in the sole. It's also important that the leading edge of the cap iron mate tightly

A BLOCK PLANE IS A HANDY TRIMMING TOOL.
Conveniently held in one hand, a block plane can pare the end grain of a stile in a frame and true up hard-to-get-at places.

CHAMFER ADDS A FINISHED LOOK TO PIECES.
With a block plane, you can relieve edges and corners to make them easier on the hands and on the eyes. Here, the author chamfers a cypress door frame.

Five Steps to Tune Your Plane

A tune-up will improve any plane's performance. Sadly, many new planes need this more than old ones. Manufacturers often machine the sole before the casting is fully cured, which can leave the sole twisted or cupped. Before using a plane, I correct these problems by following an easy, five-step tune-up procedure.

1) FLATTEN THE SOLE

To check the sole for flatness, I install the blade 1/64 in. short of the sole and tension the lever cap as if I'm about to plane. Then, with a strong light shining from behind, I drag a straightedge along the sole diagonally while looking along the bottom. Where light is peeking through, I draw lines across the sole with a permanent marker. Then I hold the sole to the platen of my 6x48 stationary belt sander. I use a worn 120- or 150-grit belt. If you don't have a stationary sander, you can make a fixture for a portable belt sander (see the left photo on the facing page).

After less than a minute of steady pressure, I check my progress. The disappearing lines tell me how I'm doing. I make sure that, at the least, the area just in front of the throat is flat. By installing an ultra-fine belt, you can polish the sole.

2) SHARPEN THE BLADE

To sharpen my irons, I mount an old 150- or 180-grit aluminum oxide belt to my sander. Using a protractor, I check the blade's existing bevel for its proximity to 25°, so I know whether to adjust the angle when sanding. Don't worry about being exact. Sharpness is far more important than a bevel at exactly 25°. I darken the bevel with a marker and draw cross lines using a square on the blade's back, behind the edge. Now I can see where I'm working and which way to tilt the blade. While I'm set up, I bring out all my plane irons and sharpen them too.

After flattening the back of the iron and dressing the bevel, I grind both surfaces on a soft Arkansas stone that's lubricated with Neats-foot or glove oil, which I get at a local Kmart or sporting-goods store. I can go directly to this step if I haven't let the blade get too dull.

To find the proper angle, I touch the thick part of the bevel and then tilt the blade forward until oil squishes out from under the tip. I usually tilt up a bit more (about 5°)

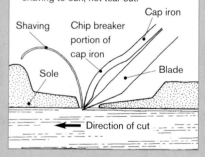

Detail A: Cap-Iron Function

With the cap iron set close to the tip of the blade, you can take a fine cut without tearout. The chip breaker forces the shaving to curl, not tear out.

Shaving — Chip breaker portion of cap iron — Cap iron — Blade — Sole — Direction of cut

Bench-Plane Adjustments

A cutaway view of a Bailey-style smoothing plane shows what the cap iron does (detail A) and what happens to a shaving when the throat is small (detail B).

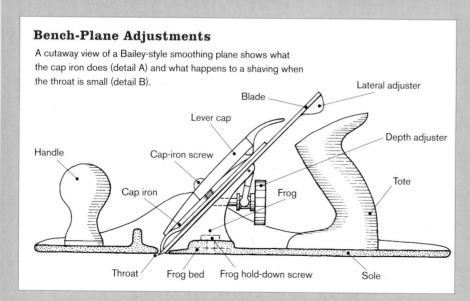

Blade — Lever cap — Lateral adjuster — Handle — Cap-iron screw — Depth adjuster — Cap iron — Frog — Tote — Throat — Frog bed — Frog hold-down screw — Sole

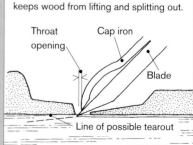

Detail B: Planing with a Small Throat

Down pressure of throat's leading edge keeps wood from lifting and splitting out.

Throat opening — Cap iron — Blade — Line of possible tearout

BELT SANDER DRESSES PLANE PARTS. A simple fixture allows Hanson to clamp his belt sander on its side with the trigger on. He trues up the leading edge of a cap iron, so it mates tightly to the blade, preventing shavings from clogging the tool.

TO TOUCH UP BLADE EDGES QUICKLY, Hanson uses oilstones lubricated with Neatsfoot oil. Without losing much planing time, he can dress an edge before it gets dull. He uses a soft Arkansas stone and then a black oilstone for a surgical edge.

POWER DRILL MAKES A PORTABLE HONER. By clamping his electric drill to a worktable and chucking in a polishing wheel, Hanson creates a makeshift honing station. Used like a buffing wheel, the setup works well in the shop or at a job site.

to create a microbevel. You'll hear a slightly higher pitch as you reach the tip. Following the Arkansas stone, I use a black oilstone. Alternating between the back and the bevel on the last strokes eliminates any wire edge.

An optional last step is honing. I rig up a fixture to hold my electric drill (see the right photo above). Holding the bevel of the blade to a polishing wheel, I make sure I'm at the correct angle. While honing, I apply buffing compound to the wheel occasionally and cool the blade with water from a spray bottle.

3) SEAT THE BLADE

Plane chatter usually is caused by poorly machined areas in the frog bed or gunk between the bed and the blade. On better planes, I unscrew and lift out the adjustable frog. If cleaning the bed doesn't seat the blade, then I grind the bed flat, like the sole. Other styles of planes are trickier. I have to reach inside with a bastard file and flatten the whole bed without rounding it at the back of the throat.

With the first three tune-up steps done, a plane can cut smoothly with the grain. But because I'm planing against the grain half the time, I usually take the tune-up two steps further to reduce tearout.

4) DRESS THE CAP IRON

A cap iron has a sinuous-looking chip breaker that acts like a speed bump to prevent shavings from shooting up the ramp as the blade is shearing off wood. The leading edge of the cap iron should contact the flat side of the blade tightly to prevent shavings from getting clogged between the two. To dress the cap-iron edge (I undercut it a bit), I use a file and my belt sander. I polish the chip breaker, so the shavings will glide over it. And I ease the front of the lever cap with a file, so there's not an abrupt junction between it and the top of the cap iron.

5) ADJUST THE THROAT

On a bench plane, the front of the throat holds the shaving down and forces it around a sharp bend. The smaller the throat opening, the tighter the turn and the better the

resistance to tearout. With a small throat, about the worst you will get is shallow, misdemeanor damage instead of felony tearout.

On a block plane with an adjustable throat plate, I decrease the throat to the smallest opening that won't choke on chips. For bench planes, I experiment with moving the frog and setting the blade depth. The blade isn't supported as well when you move it away from the back of the throat. Because of this, thin blades often chatter. I fix that by using a thick blade. I can usually guess the right combination of adjustments to get a small throat. However, because I've reduced the depth of cut, I've incurred a multi-stroke penalty, meaning that the job will take longer to finish. That's why I set up a second smoothing plane with a larger throat for rougher work.

To reduce plane-to-wood friction, I wax the sole with a candle. When you're prepping wood for glue-up or finishing, though, clean off the wax with mineral spirits before you make the last few passes.

to the flat side of the blade (see the sidebar on pp. 20–21).

To joint a pair of boards for glue-up, I first run the mating edges over the power jointer. This usually leaves a bit of snipe on the end. Next I clamp one board into the bench vise and balance the second on top to see how the two butt. I look for areas of no contact and mark high spots on the sides. Lifting the top board off, I draw pencil lines across the edge of the bottom board every inch or so. The idea isn't to plane off the pencil lines, but to use them as indicators. I plane the high areas and leave the low ones. The disappearing marks let me know where and how deeply I'm cutting and whether the blade is sitting level.

A block plane is a great multipurpose tool Block planes are little gems. If I were stranded on a desert island and could only own one plane, I'd have a block plane. They've been around a long time but were dormant in many tool chests for years—until British Arts and Crafts woodworkers reintroduced exposed joinery in furniture at the turn of the 20th century. Block planes are ideal for trimming the end grain of through-tenons and dovetails. A block plane's absence of a cap iron and its easy-to-remove lever cap make it the fastest plane to sharpen and put back into service. That makes it a good choice any time you think you might nick the blade on an embedded nail or gum up the blade with old paint.

A block plane's blade sits upside down in the plane—at a 20° slope in a standard block plane or a 12½° angle in a low-angle block plane. With the blade inverted, there's no place to fit a cap iron. To control tearout, you need to adjust the cutter depth and throat opening carefully and recheck it often. The better models have adjustable throats. Changing the direction of your strokes and the amount that you skew the tool also improves the cut.

Block planes work well as one-handed tools. When a workpiece needs a quick swipe and I can steady it with one hand and plane with the other, I use a block plane (see the top photo on p. 19). I like the low-angle variety best because it cuts plywood, fiberboard, plastics, and laminates cleaner than other planes. Freshly sharpened, a block plane can trim projecting plugs and tenons without fracturing the wood fibers below the surface. Block planes also can chamfer crisply (see the bottom photo on p. 19).

A bullnose plane refines joinery and gets into corners—Once you're hooked on the first three planes, you'll soon add a bullnose plane, which is actually a shoulder plane with a short, stout nose. Because the body of this plane is square, it does a great job on tenon shoulders and cheeks, and in dadoes and rabbets (see the photo on the facing page).

I prefer Stanley and Record models because they are a combination shoulder and chisel plane. You can buy other bullnose planes for around $20, but they lack a removable front piece to make it easier to work in tight quarters, and they don't have a screw for adjusting blade depth for making ultra-fine cuts.

Like a block plane, a bullnose plane has its blade bevel-side up. But unlike a block plane, a bullnose plane is very demanding to set right. More than any other plane I own, the bullnose has to be adjusted carefully to coax out its peak performance. I hone the straight bevel of the blade razor sharp with perfectly square corners. The cutting edge and the sides of the blade must align with (or be just a hair over) the bottom and sides of the plane. Otherwise, you'll get stepped cuts that will slowly drive you out of a corner and out of square. I grind about a 10° bevel on each side of the blade.

Bullnose planes are great for several things: truing up the rabbets in a carcase to receive the back of the cabinet, beveling an

A BULLNOSE CHISEL PLANE CUTS INTO A CORNER. **After routing rabbets in a padauk mirror frame, the author uses a Record bullnose plane to clean up the rabbets inside the mitered corners. With the nose removed, it works just like a chisel.**

edge near an adjacent surface, trimming corners in mitered frames or shaving down fat tenons. Further, you can widen a rabbet or dado by extending the blade past the side of the body to scrape the sidewall lightly. Last, but not least, with the front shoe removed, you can plane right up to a corner or joint. It's like using a chisel in a steadying jig. This is helpful for things like cleaning up the rabbet for the glass in a mirror frame (see the photo above).

Other Handplanes Worth Honorable Mention

Besides the four planes mentioned, I have another standby plane in my trusty collection: a Stanley Multiplane. Though I use it less often, it's handy for shaping moldings that router bits can't duplicate and getting into places that bits can't reach. Because a Multiplane (a No. 45 or the less-common No. 55) has a fence and rides on rails instead of a continuous sole, it is more involved to use than other planes.

It's also worth mentioning rabbet and dado planes, which do what their names suggest. Rabbet planes can have one or both sides of the blade flush to its sides, and, like a Multiplane, a rabbet plane comes with a fence and a depth gauge. By making their own paths, dado planes can work below a surface to plow a groove or dado. Good rabbet and dado planes are expensive. But because they do their jobs so well, it's worth hunting around for them at flea markets.

SVEN HANSON is a woodworker and professional carpenter in Albuquerque, N. M.

Three Bench Planes

BY MICHAEL DUNBAR

Last month, I pulled into a hardwood dealer's lot and parked next to a woodworker's van. On the van, above the guy's name, was his logo: the silhouette of a bench plane. I wasn't being catty, but I wondered if he knew how to use a handplane. The reality is that most woodworkers do not know how to use one. That's too bad, for these are the most useful and versatile tools in the shop.

Bench planes are so important to woodworking that Mr. Woodworker-in-the-parking-lot is hardly the only one to have it as a logo. The silhouette of a bench plane is used everywhere. Numerous catalogs and other woodworking companies use it. The bench plane implies craftsmanship not only to woodworkers but also to customers.

Ironically, most woodworkers do own a plane even if they can't use it. Around here, we joke about the "requisite plane" that is found in nearly every shop because woodworkers know intuitively that they should own one. For my chair-making classes, I give students a list of tools to bring. The list includes a handplane. So we get to see

examples of these requisite planes every two weeks. Usually they are not tuned and are covered with dust. Their blades are dull, sometimes rusty, and often upside down. Many are still in their original boxes.

Some woodworkers are self-conscious about their lack of knowledge about handplanes and feel they should be able to incorporate planes into their work. Well, they should. The handplane is the king of woodworking tools. It can do more jobs than any other tool I can think of. Any shop that is not mass-producing and does not use planes is doing many jobs in ways that are complicated, clumsy, noisy, dusty, and inefficient.

Just as the name implies, bench planes are most frequently used for bench work. (The smaller block plane is, possibly, handy enough that it warrants its own discussion in a future column.) Bench planes were originally made of wood, and some—mostly European—still are. Although wood planes are excellent tools, cast-iron ones are far more common, and they are easier to learn to use. The plane we all recognize—the one commonly used as an advertising logo—was developed by an American inventor named Leonard Bailey about the time of the Civil War. Later, Stanley Rule and Level acquired Bailey's patterns and displayed the name Bailey prominently on its planes.

Planes are Sharpened According to Their Use

The cutting edge of a plane is sharpened based on the job the plane is intended to do. The cutting edge of a new cutter is ground square to the sides. This shape is intended for the edges of boards, such as when jointing. However, this shape will not work on a surface that is wider than the cutter. The square corners will dig into the wood, creating an ugly track with a square ridge on both sides. The plane may also choke when face-planing. A cutting edge intended for use on the surface of a board has to be crested—how much depends on function. A curved edge will cut a chip that is thicker in the middle and tapers out to nothing on the edges. You can see this clearly if you unroll the chip and hold it up to a light.

AFTER THE JACK, USE THE SMOOTH. A smooth plane is used for the final dressing of the face of a board. The plane is especially handy for removing the marks left by jointers and thickness planers.

Numbers Tell the Plane Story

Bench planes are divided into three types: smooth, jack, and jointer. Stanley developed a system of numbers to identify its various planes, a system that is still sometimes used today. In this system, the numbers increase with the size of the plane: For example, a No. 4 is larger than a No. 1. During some

FACE-PLANING STARTS WITH A JACK PLANE. A jack plane, sharpened with a slight crest in the iron, makes quick work of dressing a roughsawn board. The telltale scalloped surface is a sure indication of handwork.

years of manufacture, the plane number was cast into the iron body of the plane.

The smooth planes were designated Nos. 1 through 4. Nos. 1 and 2 do not have much utility and are best left to collectors. The most useful smooth planes are the Nos. 3 and 4. Makers of new planes only offer a size that corresponds to the No. 4, although I saw a No. 3 in a recent Garrett Wade catalog.

As you might suspect, a smooth plane is used primarily for smoothing wide surfaces. Before thickness planers and jointers became affordable for even small hobby shops, woodworkers started with rough-sawn lumber that they first leveled with a jack plane. (Contrary to what might seem intuitive, the process of face-planing a board is started with a larger plane and finished with a smaller one.)

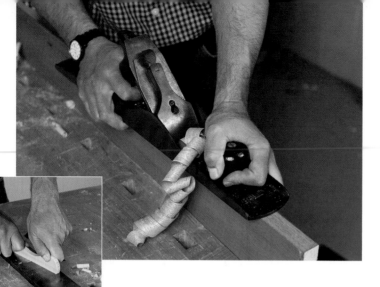

JOINTER PLANE FOR STRAIGHT EDGES. The longest of the steel-body planes, a jointer plane, with its 22-in.-long sole, cuts straight edges on long boards (right). Clamped upside down in a vise (left), a jointer plane works well for planing small or odd-shaped pieces of wood.

Planes Are Versatile Tools

Although the various planes are designated for certain jobs, woodworking is not that cut and dried. For special jobs you can substitute a plane that is typically used in a different way. For example, I maintain a No. 5 for use on my shooting boards. Shooting is a fast and sure technique for jointing and squaring small parts and trimming miters. A plane used for shooting has to have a cutter that is straight, like that on a jointer.

When making a Windsor chair, I glue small blocks to bent arm rails to create a wider hand. I joint the edges of the rail and the applied block on a No. 7 held upside down in a vise. In other words, I push the work over the plane, rather than the other way around (see the left photo above).

Obviously, being a versatile woodworker requires more than just the requisite planes. These tools are like rabbits. Buy two, and you will end up with a lot more. I own and use almost two dozen bench planes that I keep on a wide shelf under my bench.

New or Used, Buy a Good Plane

If you buy a new plane, buy the best quality. You will seldom find a good plane in a hardware store. Buy from a tool catalog, and make sure you recognize the brand.

Up until World War II most bench planes were of very high quality. Fortunately, these prewar planes were made in such large numbers that they are still plentiful. Buying an older plane has two attractive benefits—you get very good quality at a lower price. The drawback is that you have to go out and look for them or contact antique tool dealers who will sell via mail.

MICHAEL DUNBAR is a contributing editor to *Fine Woodworking* magazine.

A smooth plane cleans up after the jack plane, leaving a surface that needs very little sanding or scraping. Today, a smooth plane is most commonly used for removing the milling marks left in lumber that has been passed through a thickness planer or jointer (see the left photo on p. 25). The cutting edge of a smooth plane should be slightly crested so that it takes a wide shaving that is just a bit thicker in the middle. The resulting track is very subtle and best seen in a raking light. It creates the true handplaned finish that, curiously, many woodworkers go to great lengths trying to simulate rather than learning to make the real thing.

Jack planes are designated by the Nos. 5 and 6. Today's manufacturers produce only a No. 5. The jack plane is a workhorse, designed for fast stock removal. Before the development of the thickness planer, all lumber was first surfaced with a jack plane. It was the only means for thicknessing wood and, with its strongly crested cutter, could remove a thick chip that got the woodworker where he needed to be in little time (see the right photo on p. 25). Today, regardless of whether you have a thickness planer or a jointer, a jack plane is still a fast way to thickness parts and small boards.

The Nos. 7 and 8 are jointer planes. Today, plane manufacturers make only the No. 7. A jointer plane creates square edges either when dressing boards or preparing them to be glued (see the right photo above). To create a square edge, the cutting edge must be straight and square to the sides.

User's Guide to Block Planes

One of the tools I reach for most often is a block plane. With its compact size and comfortable palm grip, it is an extension of my hand. I almost always have a block plane within reach as I navigate through the diverse tasks of custom-furniture building.

A finely tuned block plane is a pleasure to use. Quiet, efficient, and precise, it can slice tissue-thin shavings off end grain, leaving a crisp, clean surface that no method can rival. I use a block plane for many tasks, such as eliminating mill marks from board edges and ends, shaping a radius or a chamfer on a board's edge, and fine-tuning and cleaning up joinery. Over the years, I've refined the way I tune and use this plane, based on the tool's unique geometry and features.

Typically made of metal and varying in length from 4 in. to 7 in., block planes are ideal for planing small parts and reaching into tight areas. They can be used one- or two-handed, either pushed or pulled. The blade is bedded at a low angle—between 12° and 20°—but the bevel faces upward, creating an actual cutting angle of 37° to 45° (if the blade is sharpened at 25°). The low blade angle allows for a palm-and-finger grasp and a low center of gravity, creating a more sensitive feel and greater stability. It

also puts the blade in more direct alignment with the thrust of the cut, reducing blade deflection and chatter.

Another nice feature of a block plane is that the upward-facing bevel is supported by the bed all the way to its cutting edge. This further stabilizes the blade, so it gives rock-solid performance even in harsh end-grain planing. A final attribute of many block planes is an adjustable throat. This enables you to fine-tune the plane's throat from a wide opening that accommodates a free flow of coarse shavings to a narrow slit that's capable of supporting the finest cut, leaving a smooth, tearout-free surface.

With a sharp, well-seated blade in your plane (for more on tuning up a block plane, see the sidebar on pp. 32–33), you are ready to tackle many tasks. There are five crucial woodworking operations that a block plane handles easily. A standard-angle plane works better for some of these tasks; for others, a low-angle plane is preferable (see the illustrations on p. 29).

Clean Up Saw and Mill Marks

Due to their compact size and stable footing, block planes are ideal tools for eliminating mill marks from edge and end grain (see the sidebar on p. 28). Secure the board and use a light cut. Generally, you should

BY CHRIS GOCHNOUR

Removing Mill Marks

With its low center of gravity, the block plane excels at slicing machine marks off the edges and ends of boards.

EDGE VS. END GRAIN. To plane edge grain (left), check the grain direction and use a standard-angle plane. For end grain, use a low-angle plane, if possible, and chamfer the far edge (above) beforehand to avoid splintering. Skew the plane to create a shearing action (below), and wet the wood with paint thinner or water if you encounter stiff resistance.

push the plane, but if the grain direction changes, it's easy to turn around the plane and pull it toward you.

It is important to keep the edge square. If your machinery is set up squarely, you can use the mill marks as a reference, planing until the marks disappear evenly. Pencil marks across the board edge also will serve as a reference. In time you will develop a feel for the job, enabling you to maintain a square cut without using any reference marks.

Removing mill marks from the ends of a board can be a bit more challenging because of the tough nature of end grain and its tendency to splinter at the unsupported edge of the cut. For this job, a low-angle plane is better than a standard block plane. Set the plane for a very light cut and make sure the blade is sharp. I have found that skewing the plane is a very effective technique here, producing a shearing action that contributes to a smoother, cleaner cut on end grain. Skewing the blade also lowers the effective cutting angle. For example, if the plane has a 37° cutting angle and is skewed 45°, the effective cutting angle becomes a low 28°.

Generally, I plane board ends with one continuous stroke from edge to edge. To prevent a chipped edge at the far end of the cut, there are a few things you can try: Plane a small bevel on the far edge to reinforce the fibers, or clamp a piece of scrap to the back edge to support it. Also, you can plane toward the center of the board from both edges.

Certain woods have harsh end grain that will dull the blade of a block plane rapidly. Unless you enjoy sharpening, dampen the end grain with water or paint thinner to make the wood more supple, preserving the blade's edge.

Round and Chamfer Edges

Block planes excel at lightly softening a hard edge, milling a crisp chamfer, or fully rounding an edge.

To chamfer an edge, make several light passes, rolling the plane slightly with each pass. To make roundovers from ½-in. radius to ¼-in. radius, just keep rolling the plane with each pass. After planing, slight facets will remain, but these can be smoothed quickly with fine sandpaper.

To make a rounded edge, lay out the profile on the board edge and end. Because the shaping is freehand, a diverse range of contours can be shaped simply by working to your layout lines. Begin the radius with a few bevel cuts. Then bevel the bevels, gradually shaping the intended profile. Finish with a very light cut and multiple passes, rolling the plane continuously. Final touch-ups can be made with a contoured card scraper or sandpaper.

To chamfer or bevel an edge, begin by laying out the cut with pencil lines on the board's edge and ends. Then plane to the layout lines, making sure the cut stays in the

Low-Angle vs. Standard Block Plane

Years ago, when I first tried my hand at planing, I used a low-angle block plane to level the front edges of a figured mahogany dresser. I was puzzled by the torn grain that resulted, because I knew my plane was well tuned and razor sharp. After further experimentation, it became clear that I had not chosen the right plane for the situation.

Understanding cutting angles will help you select and tune a block plane that will handle the task at hand effectively. The cutting angle is the angle formed by the workpiece and the top of the blade. A low cutting angle requires less energy, reduces friction (enabling the blade to stay sharp longer) and minimizes blade deflection and chatter, allowing the blade to slice through long grain or end grain with less effort. However, a low-angle blade has more trouble on figured or changing grain because the low angle produces a knifelike cut that tends to lift and pry, tearing the grain.

Conversely, a standard block plane with a steeper cutting angle requires more energy to use, generates more friction and dulls more rapidly. It also is more susceptible to chatter. However, these qualities make a standard block plane more valuable on long grain, where its wedgelike cut will not lift, pry and tear the grain.

STANDARD ANGLE FOR LONG GRAIN
A 45° cutting angle is harder to push through the wood and causes the blade to dull more quickly, but it breaks the chip aggressively for a cleaner cut in long grain.

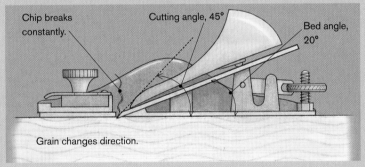

LOW ANGLE FOR END GRAIN
A low cutting angle requires less force to slice through tough end grain, and the blade doesn't dull as quickly.

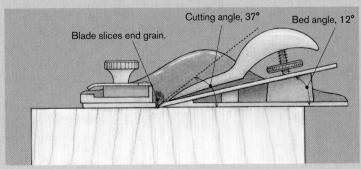

Chamfering and Rounding Edges

The block plane excels at working the edges of a workpiece, from roundovers to wide bevels to just lightly breaking an edge.

CHAMFERS AND ROUNDOVERS. Draw reference lines on the edges and ends of the workpiece. For roundovers (above), stop short of the lines with the first bevel and then bevel the new corners. Finish with fine sandpaper.

LARGE BEVELS CAN START ON A MACHINE. The wide bevels on this drawer bottom were roughed out on the tablesaw, but they were finished and fitted to the drawer with a few passes of a block plane.

center of the two lines. If you stray off course, make corrections now rather than waiting until you've reached the pencil lines.

When chamfering end grain, skew the plane's nose off the edge of the board so that the blade is cutting the grain downward. This will give a smoother finish.

Clean up Joinery

I frequently use a block plane to clean up joinery after gluing. I'll trim tenon pegs flush, moving the plane in a tight swirl and working until the blade skims the surface surrounding the peg. Through-tenons,

Fine-Tuning Miter Joints

Angled cuts from a machine tool aren't always perfect, but a block plane can adjust the fit of miters quickly.

CLOSING THE GAP. This solid-wood edging for a plywood panel has loose-fitting miter joints (left). A series of cuts makes the adjustment. The first cut (above left) changes the miter angle, and successive cuts carry that new angle across the entire joint.

Cleaning Up Joinery

For perfect-fitting joinery, make joints proud and then plane them flush with a block plane.

PLANE DOVETAILS IN TWO DIRECTIONS. First remove the bulk of the excess stock by planing along the row of pins or tails (left) with the nose skewed inward to avoid splintering the end grain. Then work inward from the edge (above) for the last few passes.

PLANE PEGS FLUSH. Plane in a tight circular motion to work toward the center of the peg.

dovetails, and bridle joints also can be trimmed flush with a block plane.

When making a dovetail joint, for example, leave the pins and tails a bit long. After the glue dries, remove most of the extra material by planing in line with the edge, skewing the plane nose inward, which supports the cut and prevents chipped edges. When the joint is nearly flush, start planing in from the end, cutting lightly until the joint is flush and clean.

Fitting a Door

After installing the hinges, use a block plane to adjust the fit of a door. Start by putting a back bevel on the door stile.

A BACK BEVEL (left) will make the next step easier. It leaves good clearance for closing and only a small amount of wood to be removed during final fitting. Next, install the door and fine-tune the fit (center). Check your progress frequently, creeping up on a fine, even gap (right).

Tune Up the Plane for Best Results

Whether you choose a low-angle or standard plane, an initial tune-up makes all the difference. Each time I tune up a plane, I follow a sensible order of refinements, beginning with the sole of the plane and then progressing to the bed, the lever cap, and finally the blade.

LAP THE SOLE. Attach coarse- and medium-grit sandpaper to a flat substrate and flatten the bottom of the plane until the sandpaper hits the entire sole. The area around the blade is the most critical to get flat. The scratch pattern will tell you how much more steel to remove.

1. FLATTEN THE SOLE

A convex or concave sole will leave the cut unsupported, causing unpredictable results, so I always check to see whether the sole is flat. Before lapping the sole flat, I also check that the adjustable throat seats well in the plane body. Remove the throat plate and check for any burrs or debris and then use a file to eliminate any trouble spots. Reassemble the plane, making certain the throat plate seats properly and moves freely.

I flatten planes by putting abrasive paper on a flat surface (plate glass, a slab of granite, or a jointer bed) and lapping the bottom of the plane. I always keep the blade in the tool, properly tensioned but raised above the sole. Begin with 80 grit and then follow with 150 and 220. You can stop there and let actual use further polish the sole, or go one step further to 320 grit.

2. TUNE THE LEVER CAP AND BED

The blade must have a snug fit with the lever cap and the bed of the plane. First remove any rough burrs or sizable drips of japanning (black paint) that prevent a stable fit between the cap and blade. Then check that the bed of the plane is free from rust, paint globs, grime, or coarse machining. The blade must have a solid footing to remain still under pressure.

Eliminate any imperfections with careful filing, being cautious not to make matters worse by being reckless with the file.

TUNE THE LEVER CAP. While protecting the back of the cap assembly with a piece of paper, sand the paint off the front edge for a snug fit with the blade.

LEVEL THE BED. Insert a small wood block into the back of the plane body as shown, to raise the file to the blade angle. Don't over-file.

ADJUST THE THROAT. A small gap in front of the blade supports the finest cuts; a larger gap is required for heavier cuts.

WAX THE SOLE. This protects the plane from rust and makes for smooth sliding action.

3. LUBRICATE THE PARTS AND HONE THE BLADE

The plane's vertical adjuster and adjustable throat will work more smoothly with a light drop of machine oil on each part. A little paste wax on the sole of the plane will keep it gliding freely and prevent rust.

Sharpen the blade as you would any other, remembering that the sharpening angle of a block plane impacts performance. Because a block plane has its bevel up, its cutting angle is the sum of the bed and the sharpening angle. I sharpen my standard (20° bed) and low-angle (12° bed) planes with a 25° bevel, producing 45° and 37° cutting angles, respectively.

I use a honing guide because it helps maintain the desired bevel angle. There are two sides to a sharp edge: the bevel and the blade's back. I take both surfaces to 6,000 grit on my waterstones.

Fine-Tune Miters

Frequently, miter joints require slight adjustments after being cut. A block plane is the perfect tool to accomplish this task. For example, if I'm mitering a solid-wood border around a center panel, and a corner has a slight bird's mouth, I first assess where the material needs trimming. Then, using a series of overlapping cuts followed by one continuous pass, I make the adjustment with a block plane and check the fit.

Even if the joint has been cut accurately, one light cut on each miter will quickly eliminate any irregularities that sawblade deflection may cause, ensuring an invisible glueline.

Fine-Tune Gaps on Doors and Drawers

Nothing works better for evening out the gaps on cabinet doors and drawers than a block plane. I appreciate how its compact size allows a one-handed grip, freeing the other hand to steady the work. Depending on the location of the door or drawer being fit, sometimes I push the plane; other times I pull.

To ensure that a door stile has enough clearance and doesn't hit when opened or closed, I recommend a slight bevel from the door's front to back. This bevel is shaped easily with a block plane, even with the door in place. Another reason for this back bevel is that only a small amount of wood needs to be removed during the subsequent final fitting.

CHRIS GOCHNOUR is a custom-furniture maker in Salt Lake City and teaches around the country.

Flattening Wide Panels by Hand

PLANE ACROSS THE GRAIN. Start at one end of the board, and work to the other, planing straight across. Skewing the plane at 45° or so may help it cut better. The jointer plane's length makes it a good reference surface, and its wide iron (2⅜ in.) allows you to make fewer passes. If the board starts to rock, tap wedges under the high corners.

BY WILLIAM TANDY YOUNG

Sooner or later, most woodworkers will have to flatten and thickness a plank of solid wood wider than their jointers or planers can handle. When I have a lot of wide panels to flatten, I take them to a local millwork shop. The big jointer and planer can do the job in minutes, and the wide-belt sander can thickness heavily figured wood without tearout. Typically, I can have all the major parts for a large, solid case-work piece sanded to 120 grit on both sides in about 30 minutes. Sanding usually costs about $30—money well spent.

When I have only a few panels to flatten, however, I stay in my shop and do the job with hand tools. The work is satisfying, and it goes quickly. It took less than an hour to flatten one side of a 16-in.-wide cherry board. With a jointed straightedge and just a few commonly available hand tools (a No. 7 jointer plane and a No. 80 cabinet scraper), I can flatten just about any panel, even one many times wider than my planer.

Many woodworkers I know own 12-in. or 15-in. planers, but few have jointers with a capacity of more than 8 in. And there's the rub. By learning how to flatten one side of a wide board with hand tools, you can

Well-Tuned Hand Tools Make the Work Fast and Fun

Planes or scrapers that clog, leave chatter marks, or produce only dust take the pleasure out of working wood. Experiences like these may send you scurrying for your belt sander. But it's not all that difficult to get these old-fashioned "cordless" tools to sing. Before you put a 60-grit belt on your sander, try tuning up your hand tools.

SET THE CHIP BREAKER ⅟₁₆ IN. OR LESS from the end of the plane iron. This will help keep the throat clear of chips. Grind off the corners of the iron on a bench grinder so that they won't gouge the wood.

WAX THE PLANE'S SOLE to keep it gliding smoothly. Either beeswax or paraffin is a good choice.

TUNING A JOINTER PLANE FOR FLATTENING

Besides the basics of plane tune-up (a flat sole and a well-honed iron with a flat back), there are other steps that will improve the performance of a jointer plane used for flattening.

The first thing I do is ease the corners of the plane iron on the grinder. As long as you adjust the iron so it projects through the mouth evenly across the opening, it won't gouge the wood. Sometimes I switch to an extra iron I keep on hand that's been ground to a slightly convex profile. I wouldn't use this iron to joint the edge of a board, but it's perfect for flattening.

I also set the chip breaker close to the end of the iron (see the left photo above). This will help keep the throat clear of chips. And sometimes I'll open up the mouth by moving the frog back slightly.

Finally, I keep the sole well waxed. As soon as I feel the plane start to drag, I rub on a little more wax. It won't affect the finish because I'll smooth the surface later. A well-waxed sole makes a world of difference in how easily the work goes.

TUNING A CABINET SCRAPER

The first thing I did to my cabinet scraper when I got it was flatten its sole with some fine-grit sandpaper on a

flat surface (I used a glass plate). I ground a 45° bevel on the blade, honed it and flattened the back, and then turned a slight burr with a burnisher. This worked well enough, but sometimes I would get chatter when I scraped.

I determined that the blade wasn't seating well, so I trued the scraper body with a mill file to improve the bedding of the blade and the fit of the blade retainer bar. I also bent the retainer bar inward so that it contacts the center of the blade first as the thumbscrews are tightened. The result is a cut that's almost always chatter-free (see the left photo below). But you'll need to set the blade for the right depth of cut. I use a piece of paper to set the amount the blade protrudes through the sole (see the right photo below).

Once I have the proper depth of cut, I tighten the front thumbscrew just until it's snug against the blade. You shouldn't have to crank down on the thumbscrew. The more you do, the rougher the scraped surface you'll leave and the sooner you'll have to re-hone and burnish the burr.

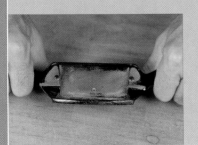

FILE THE SCRAPER BODY. Make sure the blade bed is filed flat, and file the scraper body so the retainer bar seats properly when tightened. This will help eliminate chatter and produce a better curl.

USE A PIECE OF PAPER to set blade height. With a slip of paper under either the front or rear edge of the scraper sole, lower the blade until it rests on the bench. Then tighten the thumbscrews to exert pressure on the blade.

USE A JOINTED STRAIGHTEDGE to determine flatness. Check the board once the saw marks are eliminated and the board is close to flat from edge to edge. Position the straightedge diagonally across the board to make sure it's not twisted.

still take advantage of your planer for thick-nessing. You won't have to rip boards down to size, joint them and then glue them back together. You'll save time and have fewer gluelines.

Using hand tools to flatten a panel that's too large for your jointer or planer is also more efficient and less annoying than other low-tech methods. I've surfaced solid panels with a belt sander, but I sure don't relish all the noise, dust, and vibration. I've also seen panel-surfacing jigs that consist of a router in a large plywood base riding on top of wooden rails at either side of a workpiece. My reaction has always been, "All that jig-

SCRAPE WITH THE GRAIN across the width of the panel from either end until you've eliminated all cross-grain planing marks.

building and routing just to end up with a surface that still needs a lot of cleanup? No thanks, I'll stick with my jointer plane and cabinet scraper."

Plane Across, and then Scrape with the Grain

The beauty of this technique is that I can flatten a board quickly while avoiding tearout altogether. I plane straight across the grain, eliminating the possibility of the plane blade catching the grain and lifting and breaking wood fibers. After using the jointer plane, I scrape with the grain. Because of the angle at which the cabinet scraper holds the blade, there's no chance of tearout. This lets me arrange boards for glued-up panels so they look their best, regardless of which way the grain goes. It also allows me to flatten even heavily figured wood.

After one side is flattened, you can feed the panel through your planer to take it to thickness. If the panel is too large for the planer (a tabletop, for example), take a marking gauge and scribe a line around the tabletop's edge, holding the fence of the gauge against the flat side of the tabletop. Then repeat the procedure. The gauged line tells you when to stop planing and scraping.

Once your panel is the right thickness, smooth the surface. If you're confident in your planing skills, smooth the surface with a finely tuned smoothing plane; otherwise, scrape and sand.

You should use flattened panels as soon as you can because they can warp or cup with changes in temperature or humidity. Then you'd have to flatten them all over again. If you can't use them right away, either stand the panels upright so they get plenty of air circulation on both sides or sticker them on your workbench and weight down the top.

WILLIAM TANDY YOUNG is a furniture maker and conservator in Stow, Mass.

Planing Difficult Grain

In the course of building furniture, most of your material will have nice, straight, uninspiring grain that's easy to look at and easy to plane. And most of the time you're grateful for its tame nature. But the wood that makes your heart race and your palms sweat is the stuff with swirling iridescent figure; a blistering surface that seems to be alive and filled with light. That's the kind of wood that can transform a mundane little nightstand into a minor masterpiece.

If your previous attempts at taming these stubborn surfaces with a bench plane produced only a swath of tearout, you probably resigned yourself to sanding. Well, don't pull out the belt sander yet. There is a better way. With a handplane you can save time, energy, and a cloud of dust. And it's not as hard as you might think.

Most woodworkers express some disbelief when I claim that by practicing good technique and employing a small selection of planes and scrapers, I virtually eliminate sanding—or at least reduce the unpleasant task by as much as 80%—no matter how figured the wood might be. Instead of starting my sanding routine at 80 grit and tediously advancing to 320, I begin at 180 or 220 grit.

When I work highly figured wood, my objective is not to surface the material completely using a handplane and avoid sanding altogether. Realistically, I employ handplanes and scrapers right up to the final stages of surface preparation and then resort to sandpaper to remove any minor tearout and light plane tracks. Using this method, I'm able to achieve a uniformly smooth surface, ready for finishing.

To be successful with this approach, it's important to have a well-tuned plane (conditioned sole, fitted chip breaker, and easily adjustable) with a well-prepared blade (sharp, properly beveled, and ground square). You also need to practice good technique (stance, grip, and stroke), even

WITH A WELL-TUNED PLANE and the right approach, tackling tricky figure doesn't mean sanding all day.

Bench Plane Tune-up

TRUING A PLANE. To flatten a plane's sole, the author glues aluminum-oxide sandpaper onto the bed of his jointer (top), then works the plane back and forth until the scratches cover the entire sole (bottom).

Coaxing even passable performance out of a plane requires a rigorous but simple tuning process. And to handle tricky grain, a plane must be impeccably tuned.

To take a consistent shaving, a plane's bottom must be dead flat. This can be achieved by lapping the plane on a flat surface, such as ½-in.-thick glass or a slab of machined aluminum, covered with aluminum-oxide paper. Once the plane's sole has been covered uniformly with scratches from the coarse grit, proceed to finer and finer grits. Eventually, the sole will read flat and exhibit a nice, reflective surface.

After flattening the sole of the plane, break any sharp edges with a file to prevent scoring the work surface if the plane is inadvertently tipped (these scratches are often mistaken for plane tracks).

The chip breaker stiffens the blade, reducing vibration and chatter. For the chip breaker to function, shavings coming off the board must travel smoothly along the back of the blade, over the chip breaker and up through the throat. If there is a gap between the blade and the chip breaker, it will capture the shaving. Or if the chip breaker's edge is blunted, the shaving won't travel up through the throat.

In either case the plane will choke and refuse to take a shaving.

The first step is to feather the leading edge with a flat file. Then polish it with fine wet/dry sandpaper and wax. Look for gaps between the edge of the chip breaker and the back of the blade, and file down any high spots. Once the chip breaker is in good shape, set it ⅟₁₆ in. from the edge of the blade.

With the blade assembly removed (if necessary), loosen the screws holding the frog to the plane body and move the frog forward. Once the blade assembly has been replaced onto the frog, the mouth opening should be reduced. When repositioning the frog, remember that the mouth opening must be greater than the thickness of the shavings, or they won't fit through the opening.

For any blade to perform well, it must be razor sharp. For quick but dependable results, I use a slow-speed grinder (1,725 rpm) outfitted with an 80-grit Carborundum wheel. I support the blade on a tool rest to prepare the edge with a 25° primary bevel. The slow speed of the grinder ensures that I won't burn the edge, and the coarse 80-grit wheel takes care of the task quickly.

I like to grind a camber (a slight convex curve) along the blade's edge. This light curve

when faced with some wild figure. With this approach, sanding shouldn't take long at all.

Select and Prepare Your Planes

Most of the time, the boards I work with have been run through a planer, so I'm able to do the bulk of the surface preparation with a single No. 4 smoothing plane. But

dramatically reduces the appearance of plane tracks on the wood's surface by cutting back the corners of the blade slightly. I then hone a 2° secondary bevel using Japanese waterstones, progressing from 800 to 1,200 to 4,000 and finally to 6,000. I easily maintain the camber of the edge by applying gentle pressure to one side of the blade and then to the other. Finally, I lap the back of the blade to remove any scratches.

Once the plane is back in shape, set the blade square and for the thinnest of shavings; anything more will cause tearout in figured wood.

ADJUSTING THE FROG. To get an especially thin shaving, loosen the screws on the plane's frog and move it forward, adjusting until the blade has only the slightest opening.

when you have a board that's too wide for your planer or one that has wide crotches or is especially figured, which would get chewed up in the planer, you have to thickness it by hand. In these situations, you would no sooner prepare the surface with a single plane than you would play 18 holes of golf with a single club. Milling (and surfacing) lumber by hand is physically demanding and time-consuming. Different planes are employed at various stages to minimize the effort and produce the best results.

Each plane has a single task or function that it performs better than others. Aside from their physical appearance, planes differ in their weight and the width of their mouth opening. Basically, more weight and a smaller mouth opening help a plane achieve a finer, smoother surface in difficult grain.

On rough lumber, I use a No. 40½ scrub plane to remove material aggressively and to render the board flat. Next, I use a No. 5 jack plane to remove the scalloped plane tracks and tearout left by the scrub plane. After the jack plane, I might use a No. 6 fore or No. 7 jointer plane to get the board dead flat and straight. Finally, I use a No. 4 smoothing plane to achieve a clean and perfectly flat surface.

A well-tuned smoother is critical

Because I depend on the smoothing plane to deliver the final surface, its performance must be impeccable. The plane must glide easily over the wood while removing tissue-thin shavings. It must also respond to small adjustments and hold its settings.

Any smoothing plane can be modified or adjusted to perform well on figured wood. When properly tuned, the common Record or Stanley will do much better than you might imagine. But if you're looking for even more effortless planing and are willing to put out a substantial one-time investment, try one of the higher-end smoothers (see the sidebar on p. 46).

Position Is Everything

WORK COMFORTABLY. With feet at shoulder width and the workpiece stabilized at a comfortable working height (right), you'll find that the plane will actually telegraph the blade's performance to your hands. To flatten a surface, find a relaxed stance and use a long straightedge to locate high spots that need more planing.

Regardless of the plane you choose, be sure that it is well tuned (for more on tuning up a handplane, see the sidebar on pp. 38–39). I always retrofit my planes with premium-quality blades, made by either Hock or Lie-Nielsen (see Sources on p. 46). The blades from these two manufacturers are made to rigorous standards, using thick metals, high-quality alloys and exacting heat-treating processes. These blades typically have longer-lasting edges. Put one of them in a plane, and I am sure you will notice an immediate difference in the plane's performance.

Practice Good Technique

One of the secrets of getting a good performance from your plane is to maintain complete control of the tool. The more physical effort you put into planing, the less control you have over the tool—and the less knowledge you have of what the tool is doing. A finely tuned plane will telegraph exactly what it's doing to the wood, through the sole, right up the handles to your hands. You can clearly feel the kind of surface it's leaving behind.

Make proper adjustments to the blade—The most effective way to control the tool is to adjust the blade so that it projects uniformly across the entire cutting edge. The objective is to produce a paper-thin, full-width shaving of uniform thickness. If the blade's edge projects unevenly, it will cut more heavily on one side and possibly choke or jam the plane. And it will leave conspicuous plane tracks in its wake.

Most people think the blade's edge must be clearly visible. But you're better off developing a feel for the blade setting. I rarely sight down the plane's sole for a visual reading and instead rely on my fingertips—carefully strummed over the edge from behind—to guide me. The blade should barely project below the sole. If the plane fails to produce a shaving, advance the blade a little at a time.

Stand in a comfortable position With the plane tuned up and the blade properly

SOUPED-UP PLANE. While a sharp, standard iron will do the trick, a thicker replacement iron will make it easier.

How to Hold and Move a Plane

SMOOTH STROKES. On average grain patterns, begin planing by pressing down on the front of the plane. As you proceed, shift pressure to the back of the plane.

A SWEEPING CUT. For difficult figure, such as bird's eye, set the blade for a thin cut and take skewed, arching passes.

adjusted, it's time to go to work. The workpiece should be positioned at or near waist height. The idea is to find a height that allows you to extend your reach fully without cramping your shoulders or straining your back. As I mentioned, planing is a physically demanding activity, so find a comfortable position—you may have to hold it for a while.

It's usually easiest to work near the front edge of the bench. I sometimes allow a couple of inches to overhang for better

accessibility. But don't overdo it. Too much overhang may cause the workpiece to tip slightly, dissipating the pressure of the plane's cut.

Once the work has been secured to the bench, place your feet about shoulder-width apart. If you're leading with your left foot, your right foot should be 90° to it for stability. As you advance the plane's stroke, your weight shifts in that direction.

Planing should not be rushed or frantic. Inspect your work frequently and think

Working with the Grain

I rarely sight down the plane's sole for a visual reading and instead rely on my fingertips—carefully strummed over the edge from behind—to guide me. On easy, straight-grained woods, you can get away with a slightly more aggressive cut, but as the grain gets trickier, the cut should get finer.

With the grain
When the end grain on the board is convex, plane into the peaks.

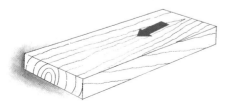

Against the grain
If the end grain curves in a concave, downward pattern, plane away from the peaks.

If the grain changes
When the grain changes direction, take shorter strokes, approaching from each end.

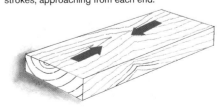

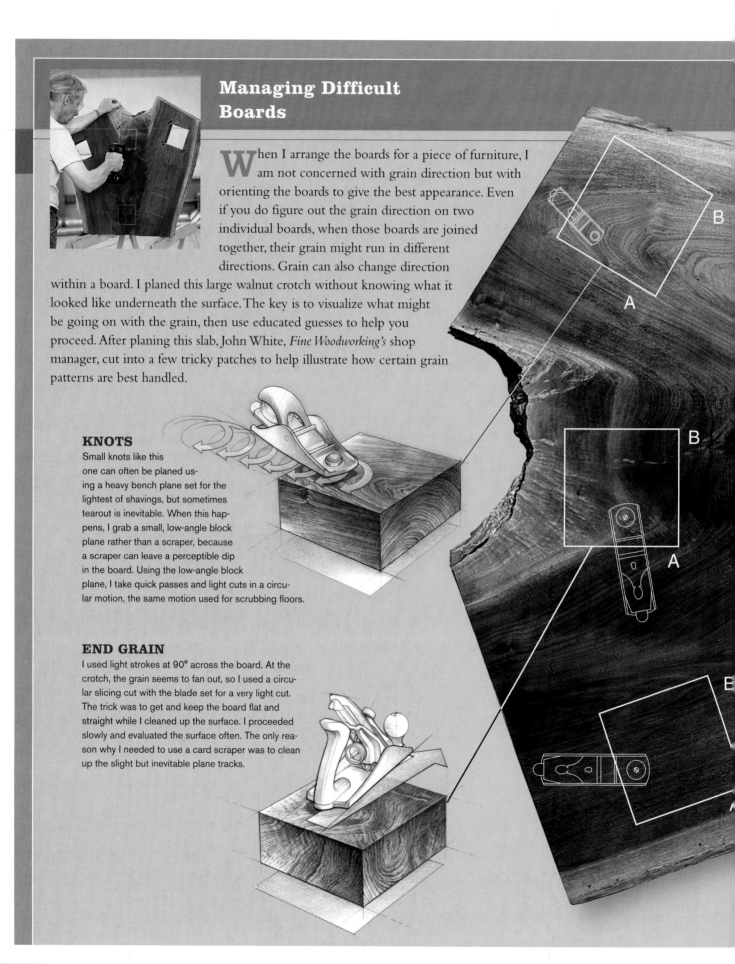

Managing Difficult Boards

When I arrange the boards for a piece of furniture, I am not concerned with grain direction but with orienting the boards to give the best appearance. Even if you do figure out the grain direction on two individual boards, when those boards are joined together, their grain might run in different directions. Grain can also change direction within a board. I planed this large walnut crotch without knowing what it looked like underneath the surface. The key is to visualize what might be going on with the grain, then use educated guesses to help you proceed. After planing this slab, John White, *Fine Woodworking's* shop manager, cut into a few tricky patches to help illustrate how certain grain patterns are best handled.

KNOTS

Small knots like this one can often be planed using a heavy bench plane set for the lightest of shavings, but sometimes tearout is inevitable. When this happens, I grab a small, low-angle block plane rather than a scraper, because a scraper can leave a perceptible dip in the board. Using the low-angle block plane, I take quick passes and light cuts in a circular motion, the same motion used for scrubbing floors.

END GRAIN

I used light strokes at 90° across the board. At the crotch, the grain seems to fan out, so I used a circular slicing cut with the blade set for a very light cut. The trick was to get and keep the board flat and straight while I cleaned up the surface. I proceeded slowly and evaluated the surface often. The only reason why I needed to use a card scraper was to clean up the slight but inevitable plane tracks.

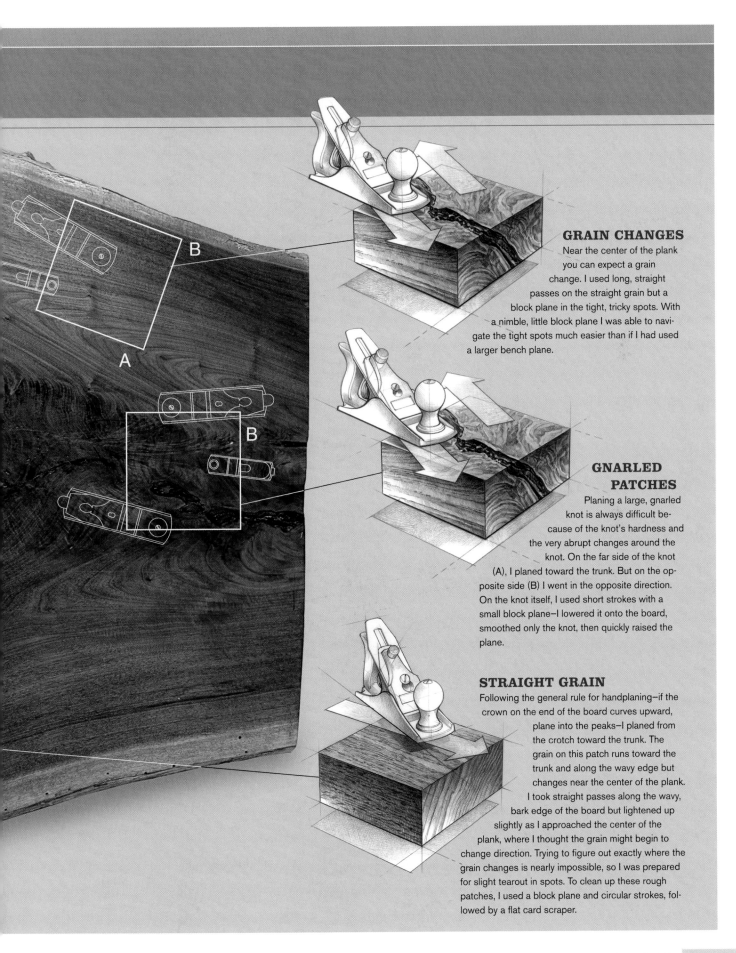

GRAIN CHANGES

Near the center of the plank you can expect a grain change. I used long, straight passes on the straight grain but a block plane in the tight, tricky spots. With a nimble, little block plane I was able to navigate the tight spots much easier than if I had used a larger bench plane.

GNARLED PATCHES

Planing a large, gnarled knot is always difficult because of the knot's hardness and the very abrupt changes around the knot. On the far side of the knot (A), I planed toward the trunk. But on the opposite side (B) I went in the opposite direction. On the knot itself, I used short strokes with a small block plane—I lowered it onto the board, smoothed only the knot, then quickly raised the plane.

STRAIGHT GRAIN

Following the general rule for handplaning—if the crown on the end of the board curves upward, plane into the peaks—I planed from the crotch toward the trunk. The grain on this patch runs toward the trunk and along the wavy edge but changes near the center of the plank. I took straight passes along the wavy, bark edge of the board but lightened up slightly as I approached the center of the plank, where I thought the grain might begin to change direction. Trying to figure out exactly where the grain changes is nearly impossible, so I was prepared for slight tearout in spots. To clean up these rough patches, I used a block plane and circular strokes, followed by a flat card scraper.

QUICK STROKES FOR FINICKY WORK. **Taking short strokes with a skewed low-angle block plane is a good way to handle tricky areas where the grain changes direction.**

THE NIMBLE SCRAPER. **A handheld card scraper honed with a fine burr makes easy work of tricky areas where the grain changes direction.**

about the next step. If you're using the right tool and it has been properly prepared, the work will proceed nicely, and the surface will improve noticeably.

Grip the plane correctly Try to keep the plane blade continuously engaged with the wood, no matter where the tool is on the board. Maintain constant and uniform pressure against the workpiece throughout the entire plane stroke. This is how the plane cuts best, and any change will affect the shaving and the surface.

By gripping the front knob and pressing down firmly upon the wood, you should produce an even, continuous shaving and leave a smooth surface without chatter marks. But as you approach the far end of the workpiece, let up on the front knob and transfer the pressure to the rear handle, propelling the plane forward instead of downward. This maneuver prevents the plane from taking a slightly heavier cut as the unsupported blade runs off the edge of the board, which could result in a board that is noticeably thinner at one end.

Try to Plane with the Grain

I compare planing against the grain with running your hand up the back of your head. Your hair grows down the back of your head, and your hand, run in the opposite direction, disturbs and upsets your hair's natural arrangement. It's the same thing with wood. The proper direction would be away from the ends.

On the surface of a board, you can often recognize the peaks formed by the grain. If the end grain curves in a convex pattern, you should plane down into the peaks. If the end grain curves downward (concave pattern), you should plane up and away from the peaks.

Now these rules certainly oversimplify a complicated subject, and they're meant only as a basic guide. The patterns and clues I just described are not always easy to decipher. On crotch, burl, or even curly wood, these signs may not be of much help. On highly figured pieces, the grain swirls in different directions.

Ultimately you'll have to rely on the surface quality left by the plane, the cutting sounds made by the plane, and the resistance encountered as you pass the plane over the workpiece to tell if you should change direction. All of these tangible clues will tell you whether the plane is cutting with the grain or against it.

In addition to reading these visible clues, you must employ strategies for navigating the swirling grain, as shown in the sidebar on pp. 42–43, as well as remedial techniques for repairing any damage to the surface.

Use a Scraper to Repair Any Damage

No matter what type of plane you have or how well you've learned to read the grain, you'll cause a certain degree of unintentional damage, such as tearout, to your workpiece. As the scope of the job becomes narrower, the tools called upon must also become smaller; smaller tools with smaller blades are used to work smaller areas of wood. These tools are also more manageable, allowing you to work very specific problem areas without disturbing completed areas.

The best tool for removing minor blemishes is a handheld flat card scraper. For a few reasons I prefer this tool over a rigid-blade scraper supported in a plane-type body. The card scraper is light and flexible, which allow me literally to turn on a dime. I can always see exactly where I'm working. I can turn it 360°, responding to even the smallest blemish or grain change. And I can instantly change the cutting angle and the depth of cut.

I thoroughly enjoy this part of the job. The nimble scraper is versatile enough to handle the sudden changes in grain direction that are the consequence of convoluted grain. It is invaluable in removing any trace of plane tracks, overlooked machine marks, metallic stains left by clamps and isolated patches of tearout.

I also enjoy seeing the lacelike cascade of fine shavings produced by a sharp scraper rolling across wood.

THE FINAL TOUCH. Once the planing and scraping have been completed, a washcoat of denatured alcohol makes any tearout apparent. Clean up what you can with a scraper, then sand with a padded backer block. The author uses compressed air to clean up between grits.

Sanding Methodically

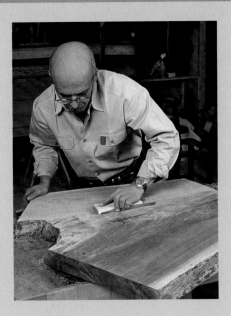

Sources

Hock Tools
16650 Mitchell Creek Drive
Fort Bragg, CA 95437
888-282-5233
www.hocktools.com

**Lie-Nielsen
Toolworks, Inc.**
P.O. Box 9
Warren, ME 04864
800-327-2520
www.lie-nielsen.com

Clark and Williams
P.O. Box 121
Eureka Springs, AR 72632
479-253-7416
www.planemaker.com

Robert Baker
207-351-1050

Kelly Toolworks
706-376-4804

St. James Bay Tool Co.
122 E. Main Street
Mesa, AZ 85201
800-574-2589
www.stjamesbaytoolco.com

Sanding Is the Final Step

Even though sanding is my least favorite part of the job, I take it very seriously and approach it methodically. First you must evaluate the surface to determine what grit sandpaper you should start with. If, overall, you think 180 grit would do, but there are a few rough areas that require 150 grit, then start with 150 grit. The idea is to produce a surface of uniform smoothness that reflects light and reveals the wood's characteristics uniformly.

Each grade of sandpaper scores the wood surface with scratches of uniform size. As the sanding progresses, and you switch from a coarse sandpaper to a finer grit, the resulting scratches become finer and the surface becomes smoother. But as the paper wears, it releases abrasive particles. If errant particles from a coarser grit get trapped between the wood surface and the next finer grit sandpaper, they disfigure the wood surface with random scratches. These singular scratches may pass casual scrutiny but will be glaring when the piece is finished.

To prevent this, blow the surface clean with compressed air (a shop vacuum could be used instead) and then wipe it down with a solvent such as denatured alcohol. The alcohol flushes the wood surface, making it easier to remove any grit left behind by the paper, and the wet surface highlights any problems that may have been overlooked. When the entire surface is dry, wipe it down with a clean rag, then progress to the next sanding grit. Proceed through finer grits until the surface has a mirrorlike sheen when you view it at a slight angle.

MARIO RODRIGUEZ is a contributing editor to *Fine Woodworking* magazine.

Premium-Grade Smoothing Planes

These semicustom smoothing planes—a Lie-Nielsen No. 4, a Reed smoother (available from antique tool dealers), and a coffin smoother by Clark and Williams are designed and produced to perform demanding work to a very high standard. Other specialty toolmakers with lines of quality planes are Robert Baker, Kelly Toolworks and St. James Bay (see Sources for company information). These planes are ready to use straight out of the box, needing nothing more than a few passes of the blade's edge over a waterstone before being put to work. But be prepared to pay for this kind of quality—the starting price for one of these tools is around $200, but they can run much higher.

Planing Corner Joints

BY JEFF MILLER

Not all corners meet exactly as planned. Sometimes, despite the best efforts at cutting and fitting, parts end up glued together with surfaces that aren't quite flush. When this happens, many woodworkers reach for a random-orbit sander. But if you're not careful, a random-orbit sander can create more problems than it solves. It sands quickly and indiscriminately, so you could end up rounding over edges in no time or inadvertently removing material from low spots, when it's only the high spots that you want to sand.

So when flushing up surfaces that meet at a right angle, I prefer to start with a handplane, which allows me to remove just the right amount of stock without having to worry about distorting surfaces or rounding over edges. I still use a random-orbit sander on occasion but only after the surfaces have been pretty well flattened with a handplane.

Start with a Well-Tuned Handplane

For this procedure to work, your plane must be sharp enough to slice thin shavings. If it's not, some extra honing and adjusting is in order.

Although you can use any smoothing plane or jack plane, I prefer to use a block-style, low-angle smoothing plane. Unlike the standard jack or smoothing plane, which has the bevel of the blade facing down, a block-style plane has the blade bevel facing up. I sharpen the blade to between 35° and 40°, much steeper than the original 25° angle. So the cutting edge of the plane meets the wood at a steeper angle than a typical smoothing plane and does a better job of cutting difficult grain. Then, I adjust the mouth so that it's close to the blade, between $\frac{1}{32}$ in. and $\frac{1}{64}$ in.

Plane Surfaces Flush

The procedure for getting the surfaces flush can be distilled into two main steps:

THIS SIDE UP. On a block-style plane, the bevel of the blade faces up.

Plane Around the Corners to Produce a Flush Joint

A glued-up corner joint that's not perfectly flush can be quickly smoothed and leveled. All it takes is a sharp handplane and a technique that steers the plane around the bend in one motion.

roughing, which removes most of the wood, and smoothing, which gets the parts perfectly flush. The handplane does all the work in both steps, although the planing technique for each one is different.

Rough Planing Gets the Joint Close

Before beginning this step, check the offset between the parts. If the parts are almost

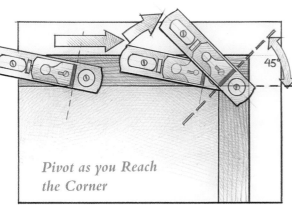

Pivot as you Reach the Corner

Begin at about the midpoint of the frame, with the plane skewed toward the center. Approaching the corner, the back of the plane pivots out. It's done in a single motion, allowing the plane to sweep smoothly through the corner.

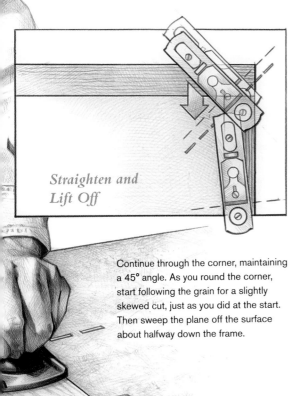

Straighten and Lift Off

Continue through the corner, maintaining a 45° angle. As you round the corner, start following the grain for a slightly skewed cut, just as you did at the start. Then sweep the plane off the surface about halfway down the frame.

flush, you can skip right to the smoothing step. But if there's a pronounced step in the joint, remove the high section first.

However, just because I call it roughing work doesn't mean you're going to take heavy cuts. Instead, you want to use light, controlled cuts, working slowly until the offset parts are nearly flush. And try to plane in the same direction as the emerging grain; otherwise, you risk tearing out the wood.

Keep the plane level and point it toward the outside of the frame. Lift the plane off the frame on the return stroke. And be careful. You can easily smack the front or back of the plane into part of the frame, producing an unwelcome dent. Once all of the parts are nearly flush, you could skip the smoothing step and immediately move to the random-orbit sander equipped with fine sandpaper. With the parts now relatively flush, the sander is less likely to do harm. But to get the best results, you'll want to include the smoothing step.

Planing Around the Corner Smooths the Joint

This step is a little unusual, because rather than planing routinely in a straight line, you direct the plane around the corner. That's the trick to getting the mating parts flush.

Clamp the frame to your bench and make sure the plane is set to take the lightest possible cut. Then, starting about halfway down the frame, plane toward a corner with the tool angled about 45° toward the center of the frame.

As you approach the corner, start turning the toe of the plane onto the adjoining piece while swinging the heel of the plane to the outside. The idea is to sweep around the corner with a smooth, uninterrupted planing cut.

You can make this cut by either pushing or pulling the plane through the corner. When pushing, start the cut with your elbows locked, and use your legs to drive the plane. Then, as you approach the joint,

A Pull Stroke Is Also Effective

STEP 2

MAKE THE TURN. At the corner, pivot the front of the plane toward the center of the frame while pivoting the back of the plane to the outside. It's the same sweeping motion used when the plane is pushed.

STEP 3

AND FINISH. Aim the plane along the grain for a slightly skewed cut, then sweep it off the surface about halfway down the frame.

STEP 1

START PULLING. At the midpoint of the frame, with the front of the plane pivoted in, hold the plane by both handles and pull it toward your body.

---

use your arms to guide the plane and push it across the right angle (see the drawings on pp. 48–49). The other approach is to pull the plane toward you through the corner, using a hand on the back of the plane to sweep it around the right angle (see the photos in sidebar above). Either way, the plane should give you a nice, smooth cut on both parts, despite the difference in grain direction.

If the parts are narrower than the plane blade, you can probably get them perfectly flush in just one or two passes. But a wider part might require several overlapping passes to plane the entire width.

Sand the Parts Smooth

As a final step, if the plane hasn't smoothed everything perfectly, do some light sanding. Here's where the random-orbit sander can be put to good use. But to avoid rounding-over problems, use only fine sandpaper (220 grit or finer).

If you don't have a random-orbit sander, or if you're apprehensive about using one at this late stage, simply hand-sand the parts. I use a sanding block, which helps keep the surfaces flat. Ideally, the block should be about the same width as the part. A block this size gives you more control, making it easier to sand exactly where you want to. A block that's too wide tends to round over the edges, the problem you've been trying to avoid.

To prevent the block from sanding into a cross-grain joint, clamp a scrap piece along the very edge of the joint line. The scrap stops the block right at the line. And by positioning the sandpaper at the front edge of the block, you can sand right up to the line.

Sometimes, however, it's easier to work without a block. In cases like that, you can create an automatic stop simply by making a 90° fold in the sandpaper.

The Techniques Can Be Used on Drawers and Face Frames

As you become familiar with these techniques, you'll discover that rail-and-stile and frame-and-panel construction are not the only places they can be put to use. For instance, they can be used to flush up the top and bottom edges of drawers or to repair face frames that have misaligned faces. Keep in mind, though, that drawers (and many face frames) are often narrow, making it difficult to keep the plane level. This makes it easier to bang the toe or heel of the plane into something you don't want dented. So proceed slowly and always hold the plane level.

Crosslap joints can be extra fussy. Rough-plane the parts to get them pretty close, then sand them. Be aware that with a random-orbit sander the edges of the sandpaper tend to catch on a narrow crosslap joint. Use a light touch, and concentrate on holding the sander perfectly level.

One last point. A misaligned corner joint is never going to be welcomed in the shop. But by applying these techniques, you'll have a joint that's going to look and work just fine. And you might just keep your nose from going out of joint in the process.

JEFF MILLER is a professional furniture maker in Chicago, Ill.

Finish Sanding

IT'S OKAY TO SAND LIGHTLY with a random-orbit sander. But use only 220-grit (or finer) sanding discs. Be careful to hold it level to avoid rounding over edges.

A STOP BLOCK CAN HELP when hand-sanding. To avoid sanding across the grain at the joint, clamp a stop block at the joint line. With the paper wrapped flush to the end of the block, you can sand right up to the line without cross-grain scratches.

SANDPAPER STOP. A simple bend in a piece of sandpaper can serve as a stop. When the bend butts against the board, the sandpaper stops right at the joint line.

Chamfers

BY GARRETT HACK

Time is hard on furniture. The wear and tear, bumps and bruises that add character to some furniture can just as easily leave it disfigured, depending on the degree of damage. How gracefully a piece of furniture ages has to do with many aspects of the design, not least of which is how you deal with the edges. If you leave edges sharp, in time they'll be rounded over and chipped away, probably not as you intended. Cut a chamfer —a bevel across the edge, however small— and the edge will be more apt to keep its shape. Also, chamfers generate interesting shadow lines that can create a sense of depth or lightness, and they offer one more surface to decorate and add detail to your work.

Look at almost any style of furniture closely, from curvilinear Art Nouveau to rectilinear Craftsman, and you'll see different sizes of chamfers. Shakers used them on the edges of lipped drawers, as a simple molding (alone or in opposing pairs) or to outline a curved table leg. Federal and Chippendale furniture sometimes have chamfers on the outside corners of chests of drawers to reduce their visual mass.

Chamfers are both practical and decorative. By cutting a chamfer, you create a new edge that reflects light differently than either of the two surfaces it joins. It catches your eye by highlighting the shape of a curve or by subtly altering a sense of scale. I've used chamfers to make large parts, such as square tapered legs, appear more slender. A chamfer cut along each corner of the leg gives it a slimmer look. Similarly, a chamfer can outline a shape and draw attention to it. A shadow line can also have the opposite effect, such as the feeling of greater depth on a shallow molding, much the same way the field in a raised panel can appear more raised than it really is.

Cut wide chamfers along the outside edges of a chest of drawers to make the case appear more slender, and you've created a place for some decorative detail. Scratch in some reeds or flutes, or add an inlay or two. Carve an end to your chamfer with a neat flourish such as a lamb's tongue or a curved stop. Chamfers are small surfaces to let go with your creativity.

Cut Chamfers with Your Choice of Tools

Unless you are cutting large chamfers or one to some exacting specifications—such as those on a tapered pencil post—you don't have to be all that meticulous about cutting chamfers symmetrically or consistentl Your eye might notice some variation in the width of a chamfer but not slight changes in the bevel angle along its length.

THE BLOCK PLANE IS FAST AND RELIABLE. **Shown here shaping the top edge of a small table, this tool is lightweight and easy to adjust. By holding one finger under the body of the plane, you can control the angle of the cut for a consistent bevel.**

In fact, some slight irregularity makes a chamfer more visually appealing.

I cut most of my chamfers freehand with a block plane, guiding it with my hands and body. A block plane will cut a clean chamfer around a convex curve; but for a really bold curve or a concave one, a flat- or round-soled spokeshave is a better choice. Stanley once made a small chamfering shave (No. 65) with adjustable guides to help cut consistent or wide chamfers around curves. But for large chamfers and clear-cut accuracy, the Stanley No. 72 chamfering plane is

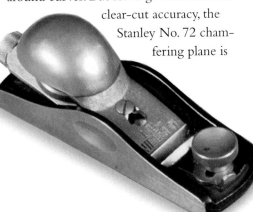

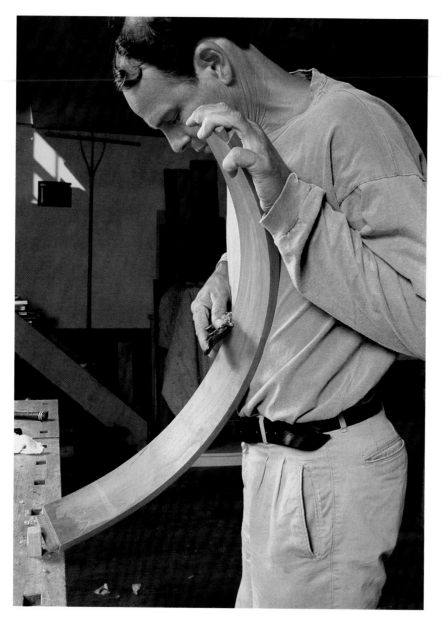

the ideal tool. It can also be fitted with a beading attachment to cut moldings or inlay grooves within a wide chamfer. For stopped chamfers and decorative flourishes, a chisel, small files, and a scraper will suffice.

Block planes Typically, I use a block plane to cut chamfers around the edges of a tabletop, either straight or curved, Chamfers are often cut at a consistent 45° bevel, especially when breaking a square corner, but that's not a rule written in stone. One advantage of working with hand tools is that you can fine-tune the chamfer angle and depth as you progress. When it looks right, stop. When you start to cut a chamfer, the first few passes let you get a feel for what it will look like and how the grain of the wood is behaving. You may need to change the cutting direction along an edge to prevent tearout and get a perfectly smooth and polished chamfer.

When working freehand with a plane, you must clamp the workpiece in place, so that you can use both hands to make steady and consistent planing strokes. One hand holds the plane in position, the other guides it from underneath, and both are somewhat locked in position by the upper body and arms. Changing the bevel angle is then just a matter of repositioning hands and body. For more accuracy, scribe light pencil lines along the edge and top surface to define the cut. If I have lots of chamfers to make, I'll sometimes use two block planes—one set for rapid wood removal, and the other for a light, polishing cut.

Spokeshaves I turn to a spokeshave when I have to cut a chamfer on a tight or concave curve (see the photo at left). A flat-soled spokeshave works fine most of the time, unless the curve is too tight, in which case a shave with a curved sole works better. The technique is the same as using a block plane, except that the two long spokeshave handles can be an advantage for keeping the tool steady and at a consistent

bevel. The challenge—especially with a curved edge—is to keep the tool cutting smoothly for the final cut. Getting the feel for the task comes with practice, learning how to rotate the shave into or out of the cut.

I rarely use the Stanley No. 65 chamfering shave, but it can cut precise chamfers along curves because it has two guides that ride along both sides of the corner, the width between them determining the width of the chamfer. (Kunz makes a similar shave sold by Woodcraft.) Being able to shift the guides is a nice feature because you can use fresh areas of the cutting edge, not just the center. This tool still requires a bit of operator control, but with the guides

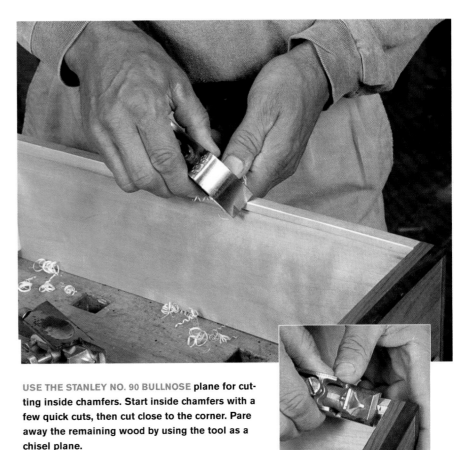

USE THE STANLEY NO. 90 BULLNOSE plane for cutting inside chamfers. Start inside chamfers with a few quick cuts, then cut close to the corner. Pare away the remaining wood by using the tool as a chisel plane.

in place, it gives you chamfers at a consistent width and a true 45° bevel.

Chamfering planes When furniture makers worked entirely by hand, plane makers responded by devising many specialty tools, such as chamfer planes, to do the work more easily or accurately. Stanley produced the No. 72 (see the top photo at left) with an unusual, angled sole that rides securely along any square edge. (You can still occasionally find this tool at flea markets and auctions.) The cutting iron and small flat sole at the front of the plane adjust up and down to cut any width of chamfer and act as a depth stop. Some wooden chamfer planes are still available; either used English versions or modern Japanese planes.

The beauty of these planes is the ease with which they will cut a consistent bevel along a straight edge. I recently used the

THIS OLD TOOL CUTS WITH THE ACCURACY OF A ROUTER BIT. The Stanley No. 72 chamfer plane was designed for cutting chamfers. The original also came with an attachment that fits on the front of the plane and accepts specialized cutters for dressing up the chamfer with beads or coves.

No. 72 to run some large chamfers along the stretchers and posts of a long trestle table, where uniformity was an important aspect of the design. As with the chamfering shave, the tool rocks around when getting started and is firmly guided by the sole only when you get close to the final cutting depth. Over the years I've found that I can work nearly as accurately with a block plane, or for longer chamfers, a No. 4 bench plane, without all the set-up fuss that the No. 72 demands.

Bullnose rabbet and chisel planes If you have a frame-and-panel door, a chamfer cut along the inside of the stiles and rails makes a simple yet elegant transition from frame to panel. Chamfering all of the inside edges of a drawer makes it more user-friendly and helps it slide more smoothly upon the runners. With doors and drawers the chamfers are best cut after assembly, but doing so makes it more difficult to work cleanly into the corners. This task is made easier by the right tool.

The Stanley No. 90 bullnose plane is a good choice for cutting inside chamfers

(see the top right photos on p. 55). The mouth designed to cut rabbets and the small sole ahead of the iron are especially useful for working in tight spots. Also, the entire top at the front of the plane can be removed to convert the tool into a chisel plane. I start inside chamfers with a few quick cuts, roughly defining the miter and scoring the long-grain fibers of one side to prevent any tearout later. I then cut the chamfer as close to the corner as I can and pare away the small amount of wood remaining by using the tool as a chisel plane. It's important to make only light cuts and to keep the pressure toward the back of the plane to prevent the iron from digging in too much.

Decorative Details Add Charm to Chamfers

You can cut chamfers all the way along an edge and miter them together at corners, but there are times when it's neater to stop the chamfer. Take, for example, the chamfered corner of a cabinet carcase that has moldings along the base and under an overhanging top. If you cut a bold chamfer all

Stopped Chamfers

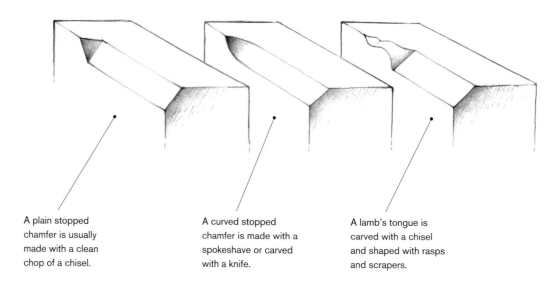

A plain stopped chamfer is usually made with a clean chop of a chisel.

A curved stopped chamfer is made with a spokeshave or carved with a knife.

A lamb's tongue is carved with a chisel and shaped with rasps and scrapers.

SHAPING A LAMB'S TONGUE. **After marking the location on the workpiece, this fancy stop detail is carved entirely by hand, using chisel, rasp and scraper.**

the way along the corner of the cabinet, that would make it run right under the top molding and behind the mitered corners of the base molding. The result would be an unattractive gap behind the mitered moldings. A stopped chamfer will prevent this problem. A stopped chamfer is also appropriate when you want to preserve an unchamfered area on a bedpost where it has been mortised for a rail. Luckily, there are several ways to end chamfers that are wonderful details in themselves (see the drawings on the facing page).

The easiest way to end a chamfer is with a square chop, but a more elegant way is to make a gradual sloping cut. You can curve this slope on both concave and convex shapes, or a combination of the two—as in one of my favorites, called a lamb's tongue (see the photo above). Before cutting the chamfer, carefully lay out where the stops are and make a few trial cuts to see what

shape fits. Wasting some of the wood at the stop before cutting the chamfer is not a bad idea. Depending upon the shape of the stop, you can cut it with a spokeshave, chisel or small files, but be careful not to overdo it.

Within wide chamfers on higher-style work, it's not uncommon to see chamfers taken one more step to molded details or an inlaid line. If you can find one, the Stanley No. 72 has a beading attachment to hold scratch cutters for just this sort of work. You could also make your own basic wooden one. Whether you end up cutting some highly decorated chamfers or simple ones with a few quick strokes of a plane, time will treat those chamfered edges more kindly.

GARRETT HACK is a contributing editor to *Fine Woodworking* magazine.

Shooting Board
Aims for Accuracy

BY ED SPEAS

Fitting miters has been every wood-worker's problem at one time or another. Whether you are making a picture frame or joining molding, if your angle of cut or your piece lengths are not perfect, you have to repeatedly shave a smidgen to get a tight joint. Although a chopsaw or a table saw can save time and

effort, it may not be the best choice for extremely clean and accurate cuts. If you use a handsaw, it tends to wander if not precisely guided. And even then, I don't know too many folks who can really get consistent forty-fives with a hand miter box alone. Trimming 90° cuts can also be a problem. A sawblade, hand or power,

PERFECT MITERS Guided by Ed Speas' shooting board, a Lie-Nielsen #9 miter-plane easily shaves a 45 miter on the mold-ing. The fence is reversible, so the fixture can handle left- and right-hand cuts.

rarely leaves a smooth enough surface. If you sand the end grain, again, you risk introducing error.

You can eliminate these difficulties by using a simple fixture called a shooting board. When guided by a shooting board, a plane with a razor-sharp edge, set to take a light cut, can accurately slice off wispy thin shavings, as shown in the photo on the facing page. And the end grain will be left with the smoothest surface possible. To use one of these fixtures, first place a workpiece against the fence, and lay a handplane on its side with the sole against the edge of the base. Butt the work up to the plane sole, and then push the plane by the work in several passes.

The shooting board I use is an adaptation of an old bench hook, or sawing board. I made this combination bench hook/shooting board so it would either hold stock while sawing (see the photo at right) or precisely plane the ends of stock. One of the fixture's unusual features is its removable 45° fence, which makes it both a miter and a right-angle shooting board. The fence is reversible as well, so I can pare miters from the left or right side, a great advantage when I need to work each half of a joint in molded work.

Making the Fixture

My shooting board consists of a rectangular base and fence, a triangular miter fence and a hook strip, which serves as a bench stop and a clamping cleat. I made all of the parts out of medium-density fiberboard (MDF). To get the 1-in. thickness I wanted, I first laminated two pieces of ½-in. MDF, about 9 in. by 25 in. Next I cut out pieces in the sizes shown in the drawing on p. 60, making sure all the corners were exactly square and the 45° angles were dead accurate, not just close.

When assembling the shooting board, I was concerned about how much pounding the fixed fence would take. That's why I

FIXTURE DOUBLES AS A BENCH HOOK. To convert the shooting board to bench hook for 90° sawing, the author simply removed the miter fence (here resting in the bench trough).

both glued and screwed it to the base. I attached the hook the same way. First I drilled and countersunk the screw holes. Next I aligned each piece with a square and glued and clamped it to the base. Then I fastened each in place with bugle-head drywall screws.

The removable miter fence registers against the fixed fence and is held down by a snug-fitting pin. I used a ¼-in. bolt with the head cut off for the pin. As an alternate, a hardwood dowel would work, but I suspect over time the pin would become loose. Because the location of the pin and the size of its holes are critical, I bored the holes with my drill press. First I drilled a ¼-in. pinhole through the miter fence in the location shown in the drawing on p. 60. Next I clamped the fence to the base in its right-hand position, so I could drill through the pinhole into the base. I flipped the miter fence and did the same thing to make the hole for the left-hand position. I chamfered the end of the pin and then tried its fit in the base holes.

Using cyanoacrylate glue, I secured the pin in the fence hole, letting the chamfered end hang out about ½ in. on the underside of the fence. For aesthetic reasons, I plugged the top ¼ in. of the fence hole with a dowel. With the shooting board together, I clamped it in my bench vise. Then I laid my plane on its side and took a shaving off the shooting edge, both sides. Because a standard plane iron does not go all the way across the sole, the iron leaves a rabbet along the base. This is necessary for proper registration of the plane. After dusting the fixture off, I finished the whole thing with oil. After it was dry, I waxed the shooting board to keep it slick and clean.

Shooting Square Cuts and Miters

To use the shooting board, clamp its hook in an end vise to keep the fixture stable. Make sure your bench is dead flat, or lay down a flat auxiliary table before clamping the fixture. While steadying the workpiece, hold the plane with a firm grip, and keep it tight against the edge of the shooting board as you take multiple passes. Use the largest bench plane you have. A Stanley #7 or #8 jointer plane works best, but a #5 jack plane will also do, as long as it has a sharp iron, squarely set, and its sole is true and square to the plane's body. Even better, you can use a miter plane, which resembles an oversized block plane and is specifically meant for shooting.

When shooting the end grain of a right angle cut, it's a good idea to knife an edge line around the board, which will prevent tearout, and then plane to the line. When shooting 45° angles, tearout is rarely a problem. In this mitering mode, the shooting board can trim tiny amounts (see the photo on p. 58). This is crucial when fitting a lipping around a veneered panel, for example, where the length of the lipping from inside miter to inside miter has to be exactly the length of the panel. Because the fence pin serves as a pivot point, you can adjust the angle of cut slightly to bisect a corner that's not quite square. Just insert a paper shim where needed between the fences. I have a stack of old business cards that work great for this.

ED SPEAS is a woodworker in Ballground, Ga.

Shooting Board Assembly

Dowel plug, ¼ in.

Miter fence

45°

Pin, ¼-in. dia.

Chamfered end

Base, 8 in. x 13 in.

Shooting edge, either side

As an option, saw 90° and 45° angle kerfs through the fixed fence to reduce tearout and guide sawcut.

Fixed fence is glued and screwed to base.

Hole for fence in opposite hand position.

Hook is glued and screwed to base.

Shooting Boards Aim for Tight Joints

BY MICHAEL DUNBAR

Whether you are making a single piece of furniture or doing a production run, you want your stock true, and you want to get it that way quickly and surely. This type of woodworking is done well using machines. But if you want to cut down on dust and decibels, or if you are short on budget or space, you should be using shooting boards.

A shooting board is a device that, used in conjunction with a handplane, will produce exact and true edges, perfect for gluing or for use in a piece of furniture. There are three basic types: the joint and square, the miter, and the donkey's ear. Each is easy to make and does its job easily, quickly, and accurately. Before the development of jointers, sanding machines, and miter saws, shooting boards were a fixture in every woodworking shop, whether big or small, whether doing custom or production work.

The joint-and-square shooting board joints the edges and squares the ends of boards. The miter shooting board trues up flat miters, such as those used in a picture frame. The donkey's-ear board cleans up standing miters: the type used in baseboard or the bracket base on a chest of drawers.

Anatomy of a Shooting Board

All shooting boards have three parts in common: a base or bottom board on which the plane rides on its side; a ledge that elevates the work to the middle of the plane blade; and a stop that helps hold the workpiece in the required position.

Lauan or birch plywood is a good material for the base because it is not likely to warp. To make room for dust that might collect against the ledge, a shallow groove in the base or a chamfer on the bottom edge of the ledge is a good idea. Still, regularly sweeping or blowing dust off the base is a good practice.

The ledge should be made of a stable wood such as pine. On the miter board and the donkey's ear, the ledge is uniform in thickness. And if you use it only occasionally, the ledge on the joint-and-square board can be made this way as well. However, a lot of use on a shooting board of this simple design will wear only one place on your plane blade. This will require frequent grinding to keep the cutting edge straight. It is much better to ramp the ledge so that wear is distributed over the entire cutting edge, as shown in the drawing on p. 62.

The stop on both the joint-and-square and donkey's-ear shooting boards is at a right angle to the edge of the ledge. However, on the miter board the stop is triangular, presenting a 45° angle on both sides.

Three Basic Designs

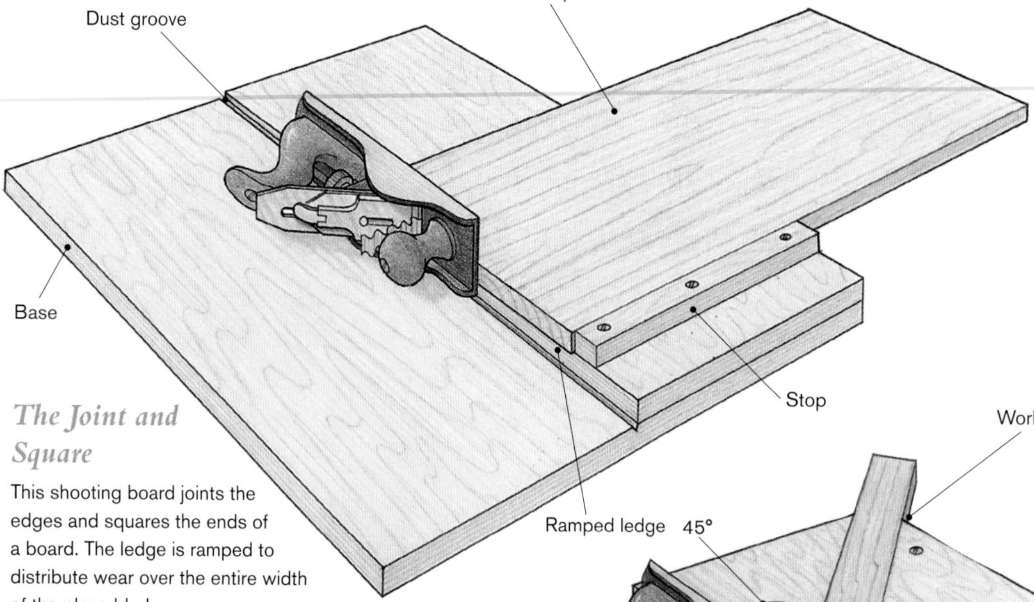

Dust groove

Workpiece

Base

The Joint and Square

This shooting board joints the edges and squares the ends of a board. The ledge is ramped to distribute wear over the entire width of the plane blade.

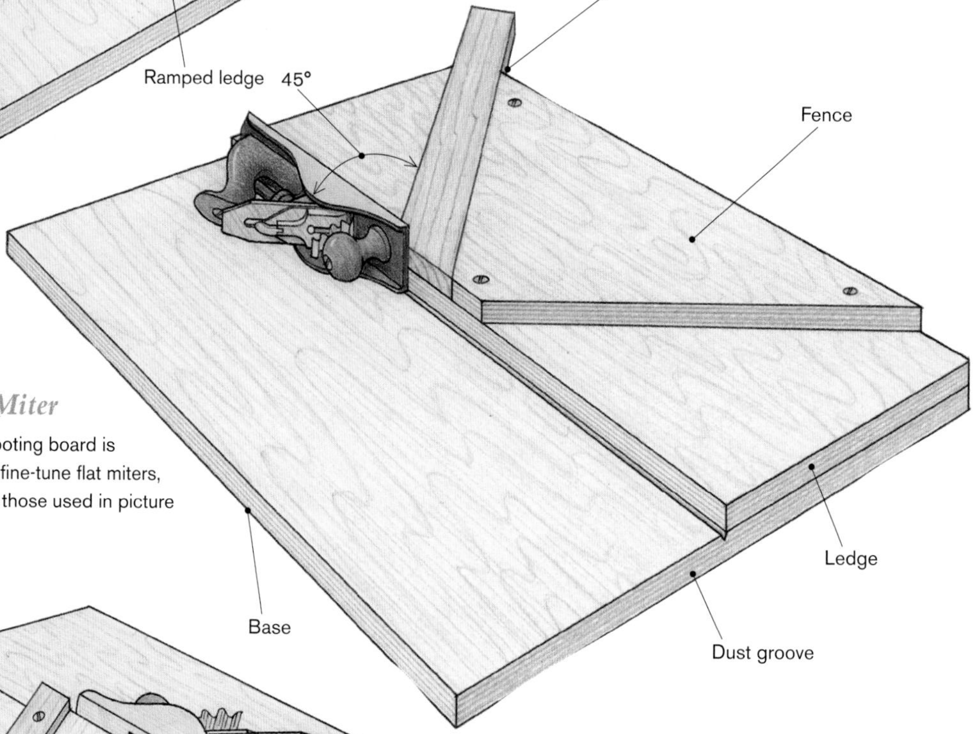

Stop

Ramped ledge   45°

Workpiece

Fence

The Miter

This shooting board is used to fine-tune flat miters, such as those used in picture frames.

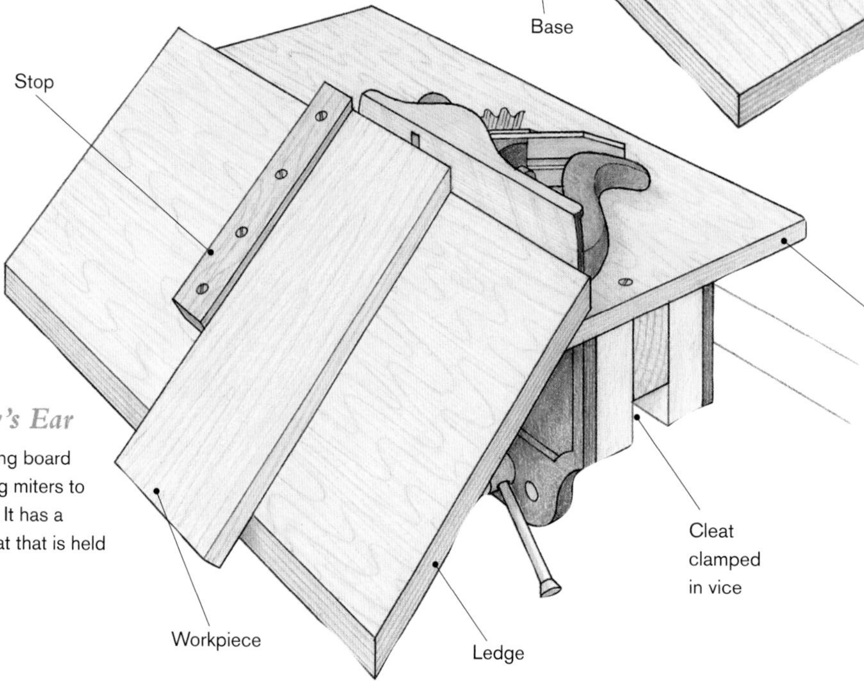

Ledge

Base

Dust groove

Stop

Base

The Donkey's Ear

This shooting board fits standing miters to each other. It has a vertical cleat that is held in a vise.

Cleat clamped in vice

Workpiece

Ledge

The dimensions of the shooting board will depend on the size of the job for which it will be used. For example, a small job will need only a small shooting board.

The other half of the operation is the handplane. This, too, should match the size of the job. For small work you might use a block plane. For large jobs such as architectural trim, a No. 7 or even a No. 8 jointer plane may be preferred. You will find a No. 5 jack plane satisfactory for most furniture work.

A Dedicated Plane Is a Good Idea

A regular bench plane will need to be reset for use with a shooting board. I keep a Bedrock No. 605 fully tuned for this purpose. Its sole is lapped flat, and its frog is moved forward to create a very narrow mouth. The blade of a plane used on the surface of a board is often slightly crested. However, shooting is done on the edges of a board, so the plane's cutting edge must be ground straight all the way across. Keep the edge razor sharp and set the plane to take a medium-thick shaving. If the plane is set too fine, you take more passes and work longer; too deep and you will choke the plane and tear out the end grain. Begin the cut by placing the front of the plane's sole on the workpiece. Also, after shooting an edge, test it with a square. If it is out of true, use your plane's lateral adjustment lever to shift the cutting edge. A coat of paste wax on the base helps the plane slide more easily.

On all shooting boards, keep the edge you are trimming close to the stop; this way there is no chipout on the far side. However, allow just enough overhang so that the plane blade does not shave the ledge.

Achieving Good Results Requires Practice

The joint-and-square board is used for preparing parts such as drawer sides and drawer ends before joining and fitting them, situations in which you have a stack of parts that you are truing at once. Joint both long edges of each part. The plane's sole will ensure that the edges are straight. Next, test the ends with a square. Using either a scratch awl or striking knife, trace a line as close as you can to the end. Place the stock on the shooting board and trim to this line. Test again for square.

The miter and donkey's-ear boards are typically used to fit parts to a project. Cut both mitered ends and try them on your project. If there is a gap, note or mark where the high spots are. Place the miter on the shooting board and trim the high spots. Test again and trim (if necessary) until you have a perfect fit.

Using a shooting board is handwork, and as such requires developing some skill. But the finished project is only half the fun of woodworking. The rest is getting there—in other words, using and developing skills.

MICHAEL DUNBAR is a contributing editor to *Fine Woodworking* magazine.

Rabbet Planes Are Real Shop Workhorses

BY GARRETT HACK

If I were headed to another part of the world for an extended stay and could pack only a small kit of woodworking tools, I would make sure I brought along at least one rabbet plane. From cutting and fitting rabbets and dadoes to making final adjustments to tenons, rabbet planes have no equal.

There are dozens of types of rabbet planes, but they all share one characteristic:

The iron is flush with the plane body on one or both sides, allowing the plane to cut right into a corner. Some rabbet planes cut timber-frame sized rabbets. Others are better suited to fine work. Still others do very specialized jobs, like cutting into corners or widening grooves cut with a router or dado set.

In 1872, the Greenfield Tool Co. offered nearly 100 sizes and types of wooden rabbet planes and an additional 38 models of fillisters (a fancier model that included a fence, a nicker to score cross-grain cuts and a depth stop). Cast iron later became the material of choice, and it wasn't long before there were even more choices in iron than there had been in wood. Many of the older rabbet planes are no longer in production, but a number of them are still being made (available through mail-order companies such as Garrett Wade, Lee Valley Tools and Woodcraft). The reason is simple: Rabbet planes have not outlived their usefulness, even in woodshops where much of the work is done by machine. Just two rabbet planes make a good starter kit (see the sidebar on the facing page).

THESE VERSATILE TOOLS clean up machine cuts and fine-tune joinery for a perfect fit.

Adding Rabbet Planes to Your Toolkit

What do you include in a kit of rabbet planes that will handle any job in a furniture-making shop? Though no single rabbet plane can do everything, the No. 78 comes close—it can cut and adjust many different rabbets.

For fitting joints precisely and paring end-grain shoulders, however, the No. 78 is too coarse a tool. For these jobs a low-angle, fine-mouth, heavy shoulder plane is ideal. Any of the larger Stanleys work well—the No. 92, No. 93, or No. 94—and they can double as chisel planes.

I would also include a No. 90. If you do a lot of fine, precise work, a bullnose rabbet can really come in handy.

Two Basic Planes for All-Around Work

For general-purpose work, I turn to a basic rabbet plane—either a Stanley No. 78 (see the photo below) or a No. 289. They can quickly adjust a rabbet that's been cut on the table saw or sink a rabbet in the back of picture-frame stock. Because these planes are so simple to keep tuned and to use, it's often possible to cut a rabbet in less time than it takes to set up a router.

These planes were designed more for carpentry than furnituremaking, so their mouths aren't as narrow as I'd like for fitting joints. This makes them better suited for less-than-fussy work. Stanley's No. 78 and the Record No. 778 (essentially the same

Stanley No. 78

tool) are the only basic rabbet planes I'm aware of that are still being made. Both are generally available. Because so many wooden rabbet planes of the same style were made, they are easy to find on the used-tool market.

Stanley No. 10½ bench rabbet plane

The Stanley No. 10, a favorite with timber framers, is still in production. With its long sole, the same as a 13-in. No. 5 jack plane, and its 2⅜-in.-wide iron, the No. 10 is a useful plane for cleaning up timber frame tenons or big rabbets in door and window frames (see the photo at left). The No. 10¼ is rare. It's the same length as the No. 10, but it has a tilting handle and knob and nickers. The No. 10½ bench rabbet plane is still being made (see the photo above). It's about 9 in. long and has a 2⅜-in.-wide iron, the same as a No. 4 smooth plane.

Bench Rabbet Planes Do Large-Scale Work

Three Stanley planes, Nos. 10, 10¼, and 10½, were designed for planing large rabbets. All three are known as bench rabbet planes because they look identical to the No. 4 and No. 5 bench planes, except for the distinctive rabbet throat. Capable of the same heavy work as a bench plane, bench rabbet planes have double irons (an iron with a chipbreaker screwed to it), lateral and depth adjusters and the same style handles and knobs as their standard bench plane counterparts.

Rabbeting Block Planes Are Suited to Small Work

For work in tight places, the smaller rabbeting block planes are handiest. The Stanley No. 140 looks like any other block plane, except that the iron is skewed and one side of the plane body is removable for rabbeting work. I've owned a Millers Falls No. 7 for years, which is a knockoff of the

Lie-Nielsen rabbeting block plane

Stanley model (manufacturers copied many of the Stanley planes after the patents expired).

The No. 140 can be used to smooth the bevels of raised panels and to rabbet with one hand. The Sargent No. 507, which has its iron exposed on both sides, is useful if you encounter tearout when planing in one direction. The only rabbeting block plane I know of that is still being made today is the Lie-Nielsen skew block plane, which is based on the Stanley No. 140. The plane has a skewed iron that's designed to give a smoother slicing cut.

Side Rabbet Plane Adjusts Width of Groove

Side rabbet planes are unusual because the iron projects from the side of the plane and takes shavings off walls of rabbets and dadoes. Stanley's right- and left-handed pair, the Nos. 98 and 99, are now out of production, though Lie-Nielsen reproductions are now being made (see the bottom photos on facing page). Stanley also came

up with the No. 79, a tool with two irons—one for each direction—that's still being made (see the photo with inset below left). These planes are great for fitting or tapering the shoulder of a groove or a sliding dovetail. If you need to take off just ½2 in. to get a shelf to fit in a dado perfectly, using one of these planes is just as fast and a lot safer than tapping on the router fence and taking another pass.

Shoulder Planes Are Precision Rabbet Planes

The sole and sides of a shoulder plane are machined or lapped precisely square so that the plane can be used on its side to trim the

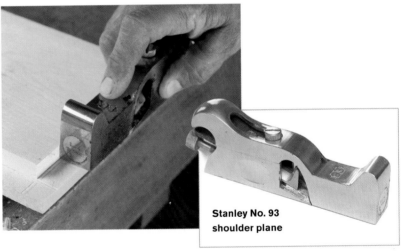

Stanley No. 93 shoulder plane

shoulder accurately while being guided by a tenon or the bottom of a rabbet (see the photo with inset above). Stanley made four versions, each progressively longer and wider: Nos. 90, 92, 93, and 94. Only the No. 94 is no longer being made (a No. 91 was never produced).

One situation where a larger Stanley shoulder plane really makes sense is for cutting a longrabbet, like the one on the end of a tabletopthat will receive breadboard ends.

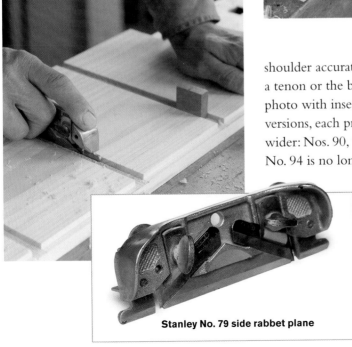

Stanley No. 79 side rabbet plane

Bend Your Knees, Not Your Back

The key to tuning any rabbet plane is aligning the iron both with the sole and with the side (or sides) of the plane. The object is to have the cutting edge parallel with the sole and parallel with, and just barely peeking out, on the side. This is one of those things that's easier said than done, and it usually takes some experimenting.

Once the iron is aligned with the side, check that it's parallel with the sole. The only way to remedy any large misalignment is by grinding and rehoning the edge. With the iron properly ground and honed, careful honing in the future should keep everything in alignment.

Skewed irons require one additional tune-up step: The back of the iron along the shoulder side has to be ground back so it's flush with the side of the plane.

The outside of the nicker or spur should be aligned with the cutting edge and should be honed knife sharp. Hone it only on the inside edge, and if necessary, bend it slightly (as though you were setting a sawtooth) to bring it into alignment with the iron.

Finally, a light coating of wax on the parts will make adjustments smoother.

FROM RABBET PLANE TO CHISEL PLANE. All four of the Stanley shoulder planes can be converted to chisel planes by removing the nose pieces, allowing the plane to cut right into a corner.

All four of these planes have threaded adjusters for setting the depth of the iron. The No. 90 has a bullnose for working into tight places, and the nose pieces on all four can be removed to turn them into chisel planes (see the photo at left).

The Stanley designs are based on the classic British shoulder rabbets, either made from steel plates dovetailed together or cast from gunmetal. In both, a wood infill was sandwiched between the two sides of the plane body, and a wedge kept the irons in place.

GARRETT HACK is a contributing editor to *Fine Woodworking* magazine.

Compass Planes

As our sawdusty world races inexorably toward a future filled with computerized machines, let me reintroduce a rather interesting old hand tool—the compass plane. Designed more than a century ago and originally intended to replace the myriad planes required in the wheelwright's trade, the compass plane is not used much anymore. You can still find new ones in tool catalogs and old ones through tool dealers and flea markets, but my guess is that after they change hands they mostly sit on a shelf again.

That's a pity, because using a compass plane is a wonderfully engaging experience, one that rewards a certain degree of skill with access to an astonishing array of beautiful curving forms.

To me, the attraction of the compass plane is practical. It gives me the freedom to create shapes quickly that could be produced on a machine only with elaborate jigging and setups. But it is also plain fun. I love whaling away on a curved piece of wood with the plane, watching the shavings curl off the tool and piling up like ribbon candy.

The shaping can be simple—like a concave drawer front—or quite complex—like a tapered, curving leg of changing oval section. I can work slowly with precision or

attack with wild abandon. The pleasure of using this tool and the beauty of what it can produce is enough to make me sneak shapes that require it into nearly every piece I design.

The compass plane (also known as a circular plane) is essentially a bench plane with a veneer-thin flexible sole. A screw

BY HANK GILPIN

GREAT PLANE. The ingenious 19th-century compass plane provides the author the means to quickly make many of the elegant curving forms that distinguish his furniture.

mechanism allows you to adjust the sole inward or outward to cut convex or concave shapes. The compass plane's blade is held in place with the same type of frog and cap iron assembly found on a bench plane, and blade adjustment and blade sharpening are also the same as with a bench plane. In use, however, the compass plane operates more like a spokeshave, with only its blade and a narrow band of the sole contacting the work. And like the spokeshave, the compass plane is more properly a shaping tool than a finishing tool. In certain woods and situations, you can get the compass plane to produce a fine finished surface, but its real strength lies in producing and fairing the curved shapes, not in finishing them.

Whatever I am making—chairs, tables, chests, or just some free-form shape—I

begin by laying out the curves. Then I cut quite carefully on the bandsaw, leaving the pencil line. Accurate bandsawing is critical. The compass plane does not do well trying to compensate for a poorly sawn line. It will tend to follow whatever wavers you make with the bandsaw. The better you bandsaw, the easier you'll find it to use the compass plane and to achieve the clean line you drew. Once I'm through with the bandsaw, however, I don't use the pencil line; I plane by eye, fairing and smoothing the curves by look and feel. Any joinery near or along the curved part is generally cut before the curves are bandsawn.

If I am cutting a true arc—a round tabletop, for instance—I set the sole of the plane a shade flatter than the curve I'm after and begin cutting. I'll shape a round top in quadrants, beginning on flat grain and planing downhill to end grain. When one section is done, I reclamp the piece and

Setting the Sole

IT RIDES ON THIS MUCH.
More of a shaping tool than a finishing tool, the compass plane is like a spokeshave—in use, the blade and only the center section of the sole contact the work.

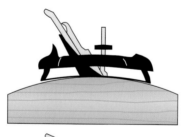

True-Radius curve
Whether the curve is concave or convex, set the sole so that both ends are just off the surface.

Changing-Radius Curve
Set the sole to the tightest point in the curve.

Cabriole Curve
Set the sole to the tightest concave curve.

shape an adjacent quadrant. I generally start shaping a workpiece with a moderate cut and then pull back to a fine cut with a lot of hard, downward pressure for the finish. I often leave the fine facets as the finished surface, but if necessary, I'll go back over the shape with scrapers or sandpaper to smooth it out.

Most of the forms or shapes I work, however, are not true arcs. Instead, the radius of the curve changes over the length of the piece. For such curves I obviously can't match the curve of the plane's sole to the curve of the piece. Instead, I set the sole to a radius that will permit it to negotiate any part of the curve. So, if I am planing a convex shape, I set the sole to a slightly flatter arc than the least curved section of the workpiece; for a concave shape, I set the sole to a slightly tighter arc than the most tightly curved section of the workpiece.

Even a workpiece with a reverse or cabriole curve, where one section curves inward and another outward, can often be shaped with the compass plane without changing the sole setting. I set it a bit tighter than the tightest concave curve on the piece and then cut the whole thing at that setting. It works surprisingly well that way, but the cabriole should be fairly gentle, and you should develop your skill on other shapes before trying this one.

Counterintuitively, a curved piece that is crowned in section (the shape of a handrail, for instance, or the foot shown at right) is easier to make with a compass plane than a curved piece that is flat in section. That's because the crowned piece is made by cutting narrow facets and blending them into a crown. On the workpiece that is flat in section, you use the full width of the blade, which makes the cutting more difficult.

Creating a Smooth Curve

A LITTLE MORE SOLE. **For cutting a true radius like this round tabletop, the compass plane is set very close to the radius of the circle and rides on more of the sole.**

Cut from flat grain toward end grain.

CROWNING MOMENT. **To achieve a crowned cross section on the top of the foot, the author starts by fairing the curve and then cuts a series of facets along it that he blends smoothly into an arc.**

Although the compass plane works like a spokeshave, you have eminently more control. But it takes a bit of practice. You must get into a rhythm with arms and body, so your hands feel the wood through the cutting of the plane. It is the balance you achieve with the plane that makes it cut cleanly—keeping the tool in a constant relationship to the wood even though the curve changes. You can gauge this balance by watching the shaving. An even, continuous curling is your goal.

HANK GILPIN is a woodworker who lives in Lincoln, R.I.

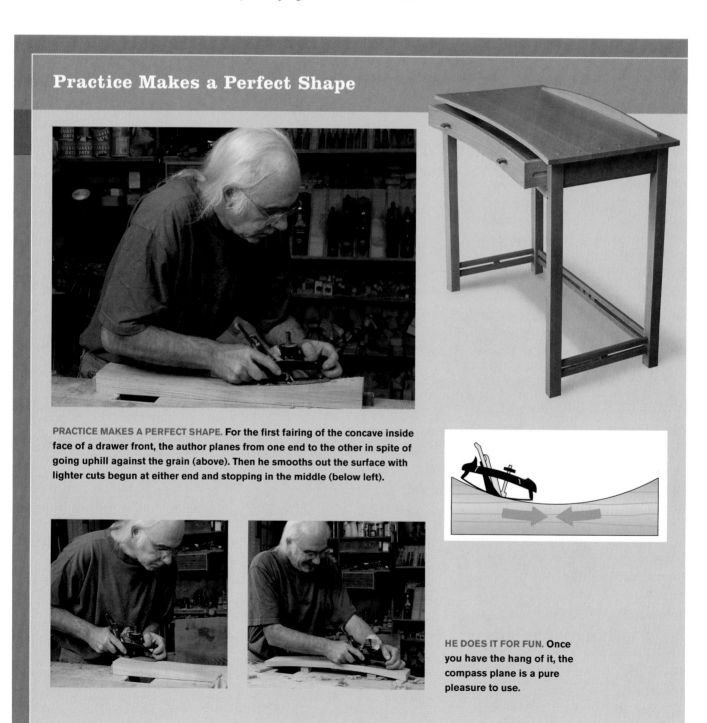

Practice Makes a Perfect Shape

PRACTICE MAKES A PERFECT SHAPE. For the first fairing of the concave inside face of a drawer front, the author planes from one end to the other in spite of going uphill against the grain (above). Then he smooths out the surface with lighter cuts begun at either end and stopping in the middle (below left).

HE DOES IT FOR FUN. Once you have the hang of it, the compass plane is a pure pleasure to use.

The Stanley No. 55: King of Combination Planes

The Stanley No. 55 is unique among planes. Produced from 1899 until as late as 1962, this majestic contraption was touted as "a planing mill within itself," capable of cutting any molding profile imaginable. Unlike wooden molding planes, which could cut only a single profile and so had to be stockpiled by the trunkful, the 55, a single adjustable body that came with more than four dozen different cutters, could produce an endless variety of molding profiles. It is truly a minor mechanical marvel, and I confess to having a soft spot for it in my heart (as well as in my toolbox).

Most often I call upon my 55 to run off a few feet of molding for a piece of furniture or a piece of trim missing from some architectural treasure. I can match nearly any molding, because if the standard cutters don't suit, I can quickly make up custom cutters from unhardened tool steel.

Some woodworkers complain that the 55 is a booby trap, enticing them with visions of complex moldings easily cut only to frustrate their every attempt to use it. True, the 55 is not a tool you master the first time you pick it up. And it's never going to replace the shaper or router table for cranking out molding in quantity. But with some persistence, an experienced hand-tool woodworker will probably find,

BY MARIO RODRIGUEZ

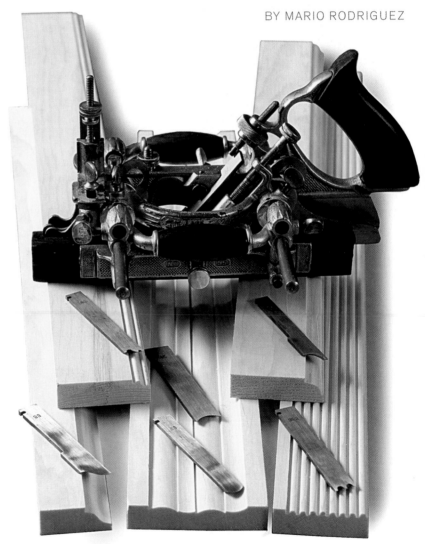

SWISS ARMY KNIFE OF HANDPLANES. With its single body and scores of interchangeable blades, the Stanley No. 55 was intended to replace the wooden molding plane. The 55 and the other multiplanes did upstage their wooden predecessors for some decades but were soon supplanted by the electric router.

as I do, that the 55 is very efficient for small quantities of molding and is also a real pleasure to use. To avoid frustration, start out cutting simpler shapes to get the hang of the tool; then you can move on to more complex moldings. I use routers for many things, but when I'm making a small amount of molding, it's not hard to choose between the ear-splitting whine of a router and the quiet whoosh of a handplane.

The cutters of the 55 are literally suspended in midair—without benefit of a wooden molding plane's shaped sole to support the cut. Every setting and adjustment to the 55 must be made with this in mind; the key to success with the 55 is to

Setting Up the No. 55 is Not a Cinch

ENGAGE THE CUTTER. A notch at the top of the cutter engages a post on the adjusting knob's threaded shaft.

FIT THE SLIDING SECTION. The sliding section snugs up to the main body. With skates that adjust up and down, the sliding section separates the 55 from all other multiplanes.

LINE UP THE SKATES. To provide maximum support during the cut, get the skates in line with the high points of the cutter's contour. Set their heights just below the cutter's.

ADJUST THE AUXILIARY SKATE. An auxiliary skate can be attached to the sliding section for additional support. It can be adjusted laterally as well as vertically.

provide as much support for the cutter as possible. This often means using more than one depth stop, fence, or skate. The cutter should be supported by at least two skates, one from the main body and the other from the sliding section. Adjust the skates carefully so they line up with the profile of the cutter. If the cutter is wide or the profile complex, the auxiliary center skate should be used as well.

The minimal support also means the cutters must be razor sharp and set for the lightest-possible cut; anything heavier will cause the cutter to dig into the wood and stall the cut, a common problem when using the 55. Another way to avoid it is to remember that unlike a bench plane, which works best with steady downward pressure applied to the front knob, the 55 cuts most smoothly when you get behind the handle and let the weight of the tool do the work. As you push the 55 forward, be certain to hold it firmly against the edge of the workpiece. Keeping the fence against the edge of the stock is essential to create a uniform profile. Unlike wooden molding planes, which are often "sprung"—made to be used while tilted to counteract the tendency to wander—the 55 must be held vertically. Any tendency to drift away from the workpiece can only be corrected with constant lateral pressure.

It is a mistake to guide the 55 by holding the rosewood handles attached to the fences. Gripping the tool there puts your hands too high above the cutting surface and too far from the main body of the plane to provide good control of the cut. And holding there also throws off your balance. I prefer to place my left hand below the rosewood handle and directly against the fence proper.

Stanley provided a valuable 22-page instruction manual with the 55. It covers all of the basics of setting up and using the plane. All of the plane's parts are identified in a clear, exploded-view drawing, and a

Final Setup, then Action

FIX THE FENCE. The fence slides along the arms and can be positioned in height as well.

SET THE DEPTH STOP. Depth of cut can be controlled by one or both of the 55's two depth stops.

THE MECHANICAL WORKHORSE IN ACTION. For best results, push the 55 from behind and let its considerable weight take care of downward pressure. To keep the plane from wandering in the cut, maintain inward pressure on the fence.

A Quick, New Cutter

To match an old molding when none of the standard cutters will do the job, you can make your own. Paint (or use a marker) one end of a piece of unhardened tool steel and trace the old profile in the paint with a scratch awl (1). (The old molding must be cut at 45°, because this is the plane's bed angle.) Use a hacksaw and grinder to remove most of the waste (2), then file the contour smooth (3). Finally, grind and file the bevel angle (4), and you have a cutter ready to be hardened, sharpened, and used. Before hardening, while it's still easy to modify, plane a few feet to check the cutter's profile. To harden the cutter, heat it to red hot and then quickly quench it in oil or water.

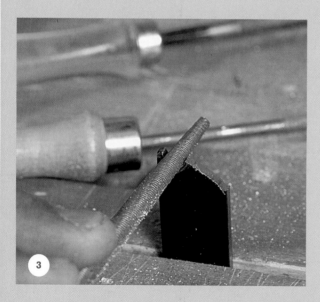

separate chart lists all of the cutters. An experienced hand-tool woodworker could probably learn to use the 55 with this booklet and a few hours of bench time. The booklet has its faults—it doesn't emphasize key points and possible pitfalls—but anyone learning to use the 55 will want to have a copy. You can get one free from Stanley by writing to: Repair Parts Dept. (Lori Goucher), 480 Myrtle St., New Britain, CT 06053.

The 55 was designed for architectural work in softwoods like pine, but hardwoods can be worked with it as well. I've achieved great results with mahogany, butternut, and soft maple. For the best results your material should be straight-grained and clear. If the material has minor faults, such as small knots, be even more vigilant about keeping the cutters sharp, and set the plane for a very light cut.

Sharpening the cutters frequently is essential, so get accustomed to the process if you want to enjoy using the 55. I've read accounts of sharpening that suggest cutters should be laid flat (bevel-side up) on a honing stone to preserve the exact original profile. That method never made any sense to me, and I don't understand how it could work. I'd no sooner sharpen my 55 cutters on their backs than I would my bench-plane blades and chisels.

Exercising care, the contoured cutters can easily be honed with slip stones while held upright in a vise. I carefully match a slip stone to the contour of the blade, then pass it over the bevel from the heel of the bevel toward the cutting edge, while preserving the original bevel angle. I start with a coarse Carborundum slip stone and proceed to a hard Arkansas stone of the same shape. My aim is to produce a burr on the back (flat side) of the blade along the entire profile. Then I strop off the burr on a flat stone. A variable-speed Dremel-type tool fitted with abrasive cones will also do a nice job.

I sharpen uncontoured cutters—dado and rabbet cutters, for instance—just the way I sharpen chisels or bench-plane blades: I start on the grinder, then hone the bevel on a series of waterstones.

MARIO RODRIGUEZ is a contributing editor to *Fine Woodworking* magazine.

Japanese Planes Demystified

BY CARL SWENSSON

To the uninitiated, Japanese planes raise many questions. Why use a wooden plane when less-finicky metal tools are available? Why use a plane that requires lots of prep work? And why does the tool require a pull, not a push, stroke?

Good questions all. Truth be told, I use both Western and Japanese planes. Metal Western planes make some jobs easier, such as flattening rough lumber, because of their greater heft and easy-to-grip knobs and handles. But when it comes time for fine handwork, I find Japanese planes to be superior over Western planes. Japanese planes come in more sizes and can even be ordered to the size you want. As with Western planes, Japanese planes require prep work and regular tune-ups. But on the plus side, shaping the sole of a wooden plane takes a lot less effort than lapping a metal tool. Because they are lightweight and cut on the pull stroke, Japanese planes are very sensitive to the touch. And finally, their thick irons are easier to sharpen because they are less prone to rocking on a benchstone.

There's a mystique to these tools, perhaps because the secrets traditionally are passed down from master to student. A teacher certainly helps. But if you enjoy the challenge and satisfaction that comes from hand-cut joinery, you can learn to set up a Japanese plane. Along the way you will pick up an appreciation for the tool. I once heard someone say that when you buy a new Japanese plane, you're really getting a Japanese plane kit. That's not too far from the truth.

TUNING UP a new wooden plane teaches you how to maintain the tool for life.

REMOVE THE IRON and chip breaker by tapping the back of the wooden body with a hammer. The thumb exerts outward pressure on the chip breaker and senses when it breaks free. The grip also prevents the chip breaker from passing over the cutting edge of the iron and damaging it.

Because Japanese planes have wooden bodies, a new one should be treated like the wood selected for your next project. Let the plane body (called a dai) acclimate in your shop, the first step in conditioning. Try to leave it alone for two to three months, with the iron and chip breaker removed. But if you can't wait that long, leave it at least a week before beginning to work on it.

Some plane makers suggest that the body be soaked in linseed oil to help seal it. I've compared bodies treated this way against others that were not oiled and have come to the conclusion that it really makes no difference. The wooden body, oiled or not, is sensitive to changes in relative humidity.

A novice may spend several hours going through the conditioning procedure. Greater speed comes with practice. With experience, a new plane can be set up in about half an hour to an hour. These are the steps in the most-efficient order (depending on the maker, a new tool may require all or only some of these steps):

1. Correct, if necessary, the edge profile and angles of the iron.
2. Flatten the back (hollow-ground side) of the iron.

Flattening the Iron

JAPANESE VS. WESTERN PLANE IRONS. The thicker body of a Japanese iron (right) is easier to hone by hand because it provides a more stable surface on the benchstone.

PLACE THE IRON on an anvil and hammer lightly to reshape it. Because the iron is a lamination of hard and soft steel, it will bend without damage, as long as the edge (hard steel) is not struck.

THE STRIKING EDGE of the hammer should have a slight radius. Small, lightweight hammers used for shaping the iron may be purchased from companies that sell Japanese tools (see Sources on p. 88).

Sole Profiles

Japanese handplanes produce very little friction because only small sections of the sole make contact with the workpiece.

▲ Contact Points

Smoothing and Roughing Plane

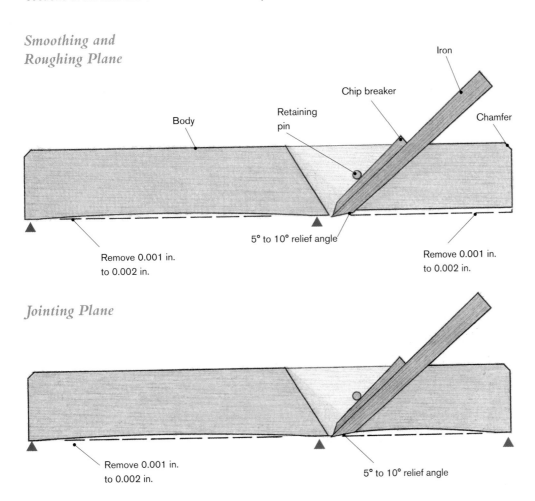

Body

Retaining pin

Chip breaker

Iron

Chamfer

5° to 10° relief angle

Remove 0.001 in. to 0.002 in.

Remove 0.001 in. to 0.002 in.

Jointing Plane

Remove 0.001 in. to 0.002 in.

5° to 10° relief angle

CHECK THE RELIEF ANGLE behind the bevel. The iron's factory bevel is 25°. The relief angle should be between 5° and 10°.

THE CHIP BREAKER has a 75° microbevel. This steep edge breaks wood fibers cut by the iron.

Shaping the Sole

USE WINDING STICKS to check the body for twist. Flatten the sole with a plane or scraper.

WITH A CHISEL, make a shallow relief cut on each side of the mouth. This area needs to be recessed anyway, and with the wood removed, it will be easier to shape the sole accurately.

NEXT, SHAPE THE SOLE. Use a scraper or a scraping plane to create a very shallow recess between the front edge and mouth of the sole.

3. Sharpen the iron's bevel.

4. Flatten and sharpen the chip breaker.

5. Tune the sole.

6. Fit the iron to the plane body.

7. Fit the chip breaker to the iron and plane body.

8. Check the sole a final time.

Remove the Iron and Check the Bevel Angle

Like classic wooden planes made in the West, the irons of Japanese planes are removed and adjusted using a small hammer. Strike the chamfer (create a chamfer if your plane doesn't have one) on the upper back edge of the body (see the top left photo on p. 80).

The iron's factory bevel is about 25°. When installed in the body, the relief angle (behind the bevel) should be between 5° and 10°. If the relief angle is greater than that, the cutting edge will be thin and hence weak. Too small a relief angle may cause the tool to ride up on the bevel. If necessary, regrind the bevel with a coarse stone or a slow-speed grinding wheel, being mindful not to introduce a skew into the edge. Don't hone the bevel with finer stones yet.

Fitting the Iron

CHECK THE WIDTH OF THE GROOVE for the iron. If necessary, use a chisel to widen it about 1/32 in. more than the iron to prevent jams.

TO FIT THE IRON TO THE SOLE, shave the ramp with a chisel. Black pencil marks indicate high points, left after test-fitting an iron coated with graphite.

STOP TRIMMING THE RAMP when the iron can be tapped into a working position. The iron is firmly wedged against the ramp. It's not held in place by the chip breaker.

Flattening and Fitting the Chip Breaker

CHECK THAT THE CHIP BREAKER is flat. Position the chip breaker over the iron and tap on the corners to see whether it rocks.

FLATTEN (OR ROLL OVER) the corners of the iron to correct for rocking. Use the same hammer and anvil used for bending the iron.

Flatten the Back of the Iron

As with a Western plane iron, the back of a Japanese iron must be flattened. Because the back of the iron comes with a hollow grind, the job is easier because you don't have to remove as much metal. Flattening, however, may also require a slight reshaping of the iron using a small hammer and anvil, which is not as scary as it sounds (see the sidebar on p. 80). Hammers and anvils with rounded edges are available for this task. Japanese irons are made of laminated steel, with hard, tempered steel along the edge and softer steel behind it, which helps absorb vibration and allows the iron to be shaped safely by hammering.

To see whether the iron needs reshaping, rub the back across a flat, 800-grit stone using even, light pressure, then examine the scratch pattern for low areas. If there are any, rest the iron on an anvil (with the bevel side facing you) and tap the low areas lightly. Because the edge is brittle, tap only on the soft, gray metal behind the lamination seam using the corner of the hammer.

The blows should push out the low spots on the opposite side. Place the iron back on the stone and make a few more light passes with the iron at a slightly different angle. The new scratch pattern will contrast with the first set and indicate whether the low spots were raised. If the metal didn't budge, tap harder and a little closer to the edge but never on the hard steel lamination. Check your progress frequently, and stop as soon as the scratch pattern seems even. Eventually, a narrow flat land forms along the edge. It need only be about $\frac{3}{32}$ in. wide.

HAMMERING THE CHIP BREAKER may not be enough. The metal retaining pin may have to be filed down until the chip breaker fits.

plane's mouth. If necessary, grind the iron just a hair narrower than the mouth opening. Begin working the bevel on an 800-grit stone. To keep the stone from developing dips, use the entire stone. To prevent rocking, skew the iron slightly to the direction of travel. A skewed position effectively makes the bevel wider and easier to control. I don't recommend sharpening jigs because the sensitivity and hand coordination learned in sharpening is good training for using hand tools.

When a burr forms along the length of the edge, switch to the next-finer stone. When the scratches from the previous stone are gone, move up to the finish stone. After honing the bevel, flip the iron and, with light pressure, hone away the burr.

Work the Chip Breaker

The chip breaker is forged with a slight hollow, like the iron, and is flattened using the same procedure. After the primary bevel (25° to 30°) is done, use the finish stone to put a secondary (micro) bevel of about 75° on the chip breaker. The steeper bevel will break the wood fibers during planing. Next, place the chip breaker on top of the iron, just behind the edge. Squeeze them between your fingers, hold them up to a light, and examine from the rear. Light must not peek through the front edge.

Shape the Plane's Sole

Unlike Western planes, the soles of Japanese planes are not supposed to be dead flat. Certain areas are flat while others are relieved, creating a wavelike shape to the sole. This shape makes it easier to keep the sole in tune because only small amounts of material need to be removed for a tune-up. With a new plane, examine the body for twist. For this I use a pair of winding sticks.

A number of tools can be used to work the sole: a cabinet scraper, a chisel (with a scraping motion), or a small plane if the

Lap the back through successive grits, up to a 6,000-grit or 8,000-grit finish stone. When making the final passes on the finish stone, work it only slightly wet and let the paste build up. This polished flat land will get smaller with repeated sharpenings. After months or even years, depending on the plane use and sharpening technique, the land will get narrower until only a sliver remains. To re-create it, go back to the hammer and anvil and reshape the iron as before. Take care to tap along the entire length of the bevel and avoid the tendency to tap too much or too hard on the corners. Doing so may produce a horseshoe-shaped iron.

Sharpen the Bevel

Before sharpening the bevel, compare the width of the iron's edge to the width of the

Learning to Plane on the Pull Stroke

Pulling, instead of pushing, a handplane may seem as foreign as driving on the left side of the road. It takes some getting used to, no doubt about it.

Begin by placing the heel of your right hand (reverse the process if you're left-handed) on the front section of the body, near the center, and grip the sides of the body. With your left hand, grab the iron between the thumb and forefinger and place the other fingers on the back of the block.

Using both hands, pull the plane across the work, keeping downward pressure on the heel of the right hand. Pull at an easy pace. As the front of the plane approaches the end of the stock, speed up the motion and whisk the plane off the board in a straight line. Because the sole is concave, a slow movement at the end of the stroke would cause the plane to dive and take too deep a cut.

Because of less weight and less momentum through the cut than a heavier metal plane, the Japanese plane tells you more about the wood you are planing. With practice and sensitivity, this helps your technique and results, especially when working difficult grain.

body is severely twisted. Never use sandpaper. Grit can become embedded in the sole. When it dislodges, the iron may be nicked. Correct for twist first and remove as little material as possible.

Next, condition the sole (see the sidebar on p. 82). Start by making a shallow relief cut on each side of the mouth. Removing this section makes it easier to shape the rest of the sole. Two basic sole

profiles are used: one for rough and smooth planing and another for jointing (see the drawings on p. 81). The depth of the relieved areas should be between 0.001 in. and 0.002 in. A feeler gauge may be used to measure the relief angle. With only a little practice, your eye will become accurate enough to judge the relief. A freshly shaped sole will be crisp at the front edge. Leave it alone. A rounded edge or chamfer will encourage the plane to ride up on loose shavings or sawdust instead of pushing them away.

Fit the Iron to the Body

A Japanese plane iron is tapered about 2° throughout its thickness. A corresponding groove is cut into the wooden body. The iron is held in place by a wedging action of iron against wood, not the chip breaker (see the bottom photo on p. 83). The fit will be too tight on a new plane. It is up to the user to fine-tune the wedge by removing wood along the ramp where the iron rests and possibly also along the groove.

First remove the metal retaining pin with a pair of pliers. Check the width of the iron against the width of the groove with a ruler or dial caliper. I aim for a clearance of no more than 1/32 in. If needed, widen the sides of the groove using a narrow chisel or file.

Next, liberally mark over the bevel side of the iron with soft pencil, permanent marker or calligraphy ink. Insert the iron into the body and lightly tap it home four or five times using a small hammer. Then remove the iron. The black marks left behind signify high spots on the ramp. Use a chisel to scrape or pare away the high spots; take whisker-thin cuts. Repeat this process as many times as needed until the cutting edge barely protrudes below the sole. If too much material is removed, the fit may become too loose. To remedy the problem, glue a paper shim under the iron and refit, if necessary. My students are often surprised by how little wedging action is really necessary to hold an iron in place during planing. Resist the urge to make the fit so tight that it requires anything more than light taps of the hammer to set the iron.

New planes sometimes come with no appreciable mouth opening. If needed, widen the opening with a chisel. A finish plane's opening should be no wider than the thickness of a piece of paper.

Fit the Chip Breaker

Measure the mouth opening and compare it to the width of the chip breaker. If necessary, widen the opening so that the chip breaker will not bind. Insert the pin and tap the fitted iron into position. With four or five light taps of a small hammer, install the chip breaker. The edge of the chip breaker should seat just a hair behind the edge of the iron. Chances are the chip breaker won't go in far enough and will have to be flattened and refitted (see the sidebar on pp. 84–85). Remove it and the iron.

The chip breaker rests atop the iron on three points: along the cutting edge and on two back corners. Place it over the iron and tap lightly on the chip breaker's back corners. If the chip breaker is not flat, it will rock, causing a rattling sound.

The next move depends on how the chip breaker fits inside the plane. On a new tool, the fit often is too tight. If so, place the chip breaker on the anvil and flatten the back corner that seemed high when you checked for rock. Both may have to be hammered if the fit is still too tight. (If a chip breaker is too loose, do the opposite and bend over the corners on an anvil.)

If you've hammered the corners nearly flat and the chip breaker still hangs up on the pin, put away the hammer. Find a file and go to work on slimming the retaining pin. File evenly so that the entire chip breaker remains in contact with the pin when assembled.

Make a Final Check of the Sole

By now it's probably self-evident that Japanese woodworking and instant gratification are mutually exclusive. But if all has gone well, a reward is not far off. With a straightedge, check the sole one more time. Sometimes, when the iron and chip breaker

Sources

Japanese planes and accessories are available from these sources:

Hida Tools and Hardware
1333 San Pablo Avenue
Berkeley, CA 94702
800-443-5512
www.hidatool.com

Japan Woodworker
1731 Clement Avenue
Alameda, CA 94501
800-537-7820
www.japanwoodworker.com

THE BACK OF A JAPANESE IRON is hollow-ground, which means only a small portion needs to be honed away. An even reflection of light indicates that the back edge is flat.

edge when making depth adjustments. Set the iron by tapping it with a hammer while sighting down the sole. The angle of the iron may be adjusted slightly by tapping the sides as needed. Always examine the chip breaker's position after adjusting the iron.

Take Care of Your Plane

A stable environment, without extreme changes in heat and humidity, goes a long way toward keeping a wooden plane true. While this is not always practical, try to keep the plane out of direct sunlight. When the plane is not in use, back off the irons so that the wood doesn't get compressed and lose its ability to hold the iron.

Setting up a Japanese plane teaches one how to maintain it. For those with patience, the reward is a good understanding of how the tool functions. And the skill and sensitivity learned may spill over into the use of other tools as well.

CARL SWENSSON designs and builds furniture in Baltimore, Md. He is also a teacher in Eastern and Western hand-tool techniques.

are firmly fitted, the plane body may bulge just behind the mouth. The bulge may be relieved with a scraper, with the iron and chip breaker in place. Finally, use a chisel to cut a slight chamfer on the sharp ramp behind the iron's bevel. The chamfer will reflect light and make it easier to see the

The Spokeshave

One of my students brought a flea market spokeshave to school last fall, complaining he couldn't get it to work. A group of students gathered as I disassembled, cleaned, and tuned up the tool. As I reassembled the spokeshave, I looked around the shop for just the right piece of wood to help me demonstrate how well the tool now worked. Across the shop, I spied a student tediously sanding an inside curve on the first of what looked to be a dozen thick, pine brackets. She'd already spent more than 15 minutes at the oscillating spindle sander, working on a single bracket. Choking on the dust and going deaf from the noise, she didn't look

BY MARIO RODRIGUEZ

Choosing a Spokeshave

A PARADE OF SPOKESHAVES. Everything about a spokeshave has been experimented with over the years, from the material the tool is made of to the sole shape to the adjustment mechanism. Stanley even made a double spokeshave (second from top left).

PREVENTING WEAR. Spokeshaves used to wear quickly in front of the blade. To prevent this, manufacturers turned to wooden wear plates, usually boxwood. Brass wear plates were an improvement, and metal spokeshaves eliminated the problem.

GOING BY FEEL. The author adjusts an old wooden spokeshave by tapping the tangs of the blade with a hammer. Then he checks the setting by feel.

KNURLED NUTS ALLOW PRECISE ADJUSTMENT. Because there are two posts, the blade can be skewed so that one side takes a fine cut and the other a heavy cut.

THERE ARE A LOT OF CHOICES, but you only need two. Most furniture makers can get by with just two metal spoke-shaves—one with a flat sole and one with a rounded sole for tight inside curves.

Tuning a Spokeshave

STEP 1

FLATTEN THE SOLE WITH A FILE AND THEN A SHARPENING STONE. Polish round-bottomed spokeshaves with emery cloth followed by 600-grit wet/dry paper. This helps the tool glide across the wood.

STEP 2

FILE THE BED FLAT TO SEAT THE BLADE PROPERLY. Check for flatness with the blade of a small square, and take down the high spots.

STEP 3

FLATTEN THE CAP IRON so it exerts uniform pressure against the blade and across the cutting edge.

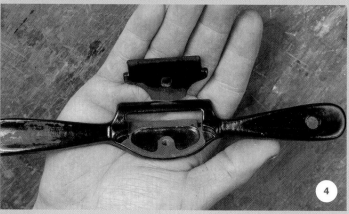

STEP 4

A WELL-TUNED SPOKESHAVE. With all surfaces that bear against the blade flattened, this spokeshave isn't likely to chatter.

like she was enjoying herself. I took one of her unsanded brackets to my workbench, and just three minutes later, I handed her a silky smooth, perfectly shaped bracket. She nearly passed out.

That's what a spokeshave can do. As a reproduction furniture maker, I use spokeshaves most often to clean up cabriole legs, shape Windsor chair seats, and fine-tune spindles. Whenever I have to shape a curve, regardless of the style of furniture, a spokeshave is the first tool I reach for.

Some woodworkers who have used spokeshaves complain that they skip, chatter, or just tear up the wood. A quick tune-up, the right grip, and a basic technique will eliminate these problems.

The Evolution of the Spokeshave

The earliest spokeshaves, dating at least to the 15th century, were wooden affairs with U-shaped, friction-fitted blades. Adjustments were made by tapping the tangs of the blade with a hammer. Because they're so light and have such a low blade angle, these spokeshaves are a delight to use.

Over the years, the addition of threaded adjustment mechanisms improved the spokeshave. Toolmakers also began introducing spokeshaves with wear plates of boxwood (which is a very dense, tight-grained wood) and brass (see the bottom left photo on p. 90).

However, the real change came with the introduction of the metal spokeshave in 1860. The blade in a metal spokeshave is flat so that it can be sharpened easily—just like a plane blade. With a wooden spokeshave, the easiest way to sharpen its U-shaped blade is on a buffing wheel. This is a free-hand operation that takes some practice.

The flat blade in a metal spokeshave also affects the cutting angle. Wooden spokeshaves have a low cutting angle, somewhere between 19° and 27°. Metal spokeshaves, however, are set like bench planes, at 45°,

with the bevel facing down. Though the metal spokeshave's higher angle doesn't cut the wood as well, most woodworkers prefer the ease of sharpening its flat blade and willingly accept the trade-off. Metal spokeshaves also eliminated the problem of wear at the throat of the spokeshave.

Choose a Set: Round- and Flat-Bottomed

Spokeshaves are available in a bewildering variety of sizes and materials and with a number of sole shapes and means of adjustment. I use a half-dozen or so different spokeshaves, but I could get by with just two metal ones: one flat-bottomed and one round-bottomed. With these two tools, you can shape just about any inside or outside curve.

The least complex spokeshave available today is set by eye or by feel, much like an old wooden spokeshave. The blade is held down with a cap iron secured with a screw. With a little practice, any woodworker can set it for a fine cut. Stanley manufactures a pair of full-sized, manually adjustable shaves, the No. 51 (flat-bottomed) and the No. 51R (round-bottomed), as well as a pair of lightweight, manually adjustable spokeshaves, the No. 63 (round) and the No. 64 (flat). The lightweight spokeshaves are smaller, so they cut tighter inside curves.

The most popular spokeshaves being manufactured today are the Stanley No. 151 and the No. 151R (and the Record equivalents, the No. 0151 and the No. 0151R). These spokeshaves have shallow metal bodies, slightly arched handles and mechanically adjustable, 2⅛-in.-wide blades.

The blades on these spokeshaves hang on two knurled nuts that travel on threaded posts (see the bottom photo on p. 91). This design not only allows precise adjustment but also enables the woodworker to set blade projection to take heavy cuts on one side and light cuts on the other, without readjusting the blade. This feature can come

PROPER GRIP ELIMI- NATES ROCKING. When pushing the spoke- shave, hold it loosely with forefingers wrapped over the top and ahead of the blade, thumbs behind the blade. Maintain even pressure on the work- piece ahead of and behind the blade.

CUTTING CURVES: GO WITH THE GRAIN

The general rule is to cut down, from high to low. This works as long as the grain is straight and in line with the workpiece. Otherwise, observe grain direction, and cut with it.

For the best results, maintain three points of contact with the workpiece: front and back of the sole and the blade.

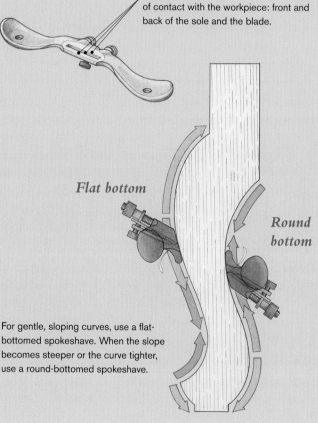

WHEN PULLING THE SPOKESHAVE, flip it around so your thumbs lead and your forefin- gers follow. Maintain even pressure on the work.

Flat bottom

Round bottom

For gentle, sloping curves, use a flat-bottomed spokeshave. When the slope becomes steeper or the curve tighter, use a round-bottomed spokeshave.

in handy. The Stanley and Record tools are also available in unbreakable, malleable iron.

Prices will vary depending on where you buy them, but a pair of even the most expensive of these spokeshaves, mechanically adjustable and made of malleable iron, will cost less than $45.

Tuning up Your Spokeshave

Any new hand tool needs tuning before it works properly. But take heart. This initial tuning goes quickly with spokeshaves. First, with the blade removed, carefully file the sole flat, and then clean it up on a sharpen- ing stone (see Step 1 in the sidebar on p. 92). This usually takes only a few min- utes. Next inspect the bed where the blade seats. If it looks rough or uneven, file it flat (see Step 2 in the sidebar on p. 92). The blade should sit on the bed without rock- ing. File and then stone the cap iron, too, so that it will exert uniform pressure on the blade and across the cutting edge (see Step 3 in the sidebar on p. 92). Mating parts in a properly tuned spokeshave are flat and seat well—that's what eliminates blade chatter (see Step 4 in the sidebar on p. 92).

Sharpening your spokeshave blade properly is also crucial to smooth performance. I grind my blade at a 25° primary bevel and finish it off on my waterstones with a secondary bevel of about 2°.

To get even better performance from my Stanley No. 151, I replaced the stock blade with a thicker, aftermarket blade made by Ron Hock (available from a number of woodworking supply catalogs). These blades are hardened to Rc62, measure a full 3⁄32 in. thick and cost a bit less than $20. The thicker blade creates a finer, or narrower, mouth opening and reduces chatter.

Using the Spokeshave

A spokeshave is a fairly simple tool, but there are some basic techniques that will go a long way toward reducing frustration and achieving smooth cuts.

Maintain three points of contact When using the spokeshave, always maintain three points of contact between the spokeshave and the workpiece: front of the sole, back of the sole and the blade (see the drawing on the facing page). A good grip will help prevent the tool from rocking and skipping across the workpiece.

The spokeshave is designed to be a push tool, and that's how it works best. Sometimes, however, pulling it is necessary because of sharp grain reversals or the position of the workpiece in a vise. I find that pulling the spokeshave is less efficient and more tiring, though, so I try to push it whenever possible.

When I'm pushing the spokeshave, I grip it loosely. I rest the handles in my palms and position my thumbs almost directly behind the blade. My forefingers go over the toe and just in front of the throat

(see the top left photo on the facing page). This grip is comfortable and provides excellent control and even pressure across the sole. For a pull stroke, I simply flip the spokeshave around in my hand so that the blade is facing my thumbs (see the bottom left photo on the facing page).

Set the blade for a light cut As with a bench plane, I set the spokeshave with almost no blade showing. When I run my finger over the mouth of the spokeshave (carefully, mind you), I can just barely feel the blade coming through. If I don't get a shaving, I advance the blade just a little at a time.

Skewing the spokeshave can help the cut, too. A skewed blade meets with less resistance and comes closer to imitating the slicing action of the antique wooden spokeshaves. And because curves always present a significant amount of end grain to the blade, the lower angle leaves a smoother, cleaner surface.

Cut with the grain It's just as important to cut with the grain when shaping curves as it is when you're smoothing a flat board. If you try cutting against the grain, you're sure to get chatter and tearout. The general rule is that you always cut down, from high to low (see the drawing on the facing page). But that doesn't always work. Sometimes you need to read the grain and make adjustments accordingly. For gentle curves, a flat-soled spokeshave works well, but for tighter areas, you may need a round-bottomed version.

★ Please note that price estimates are from 1997.

MARIO RODRIGUEZ is a contributing editor to *Fine Woodworking* magazine.

Soup Up Your Spokeshave

BY BRIAN BOGGS

The tool's name suggests that the spokeshave is for shaving wheel spokes, but chairmakers and cabinetmakers have been using the spokeshave for generations in myriad wood-shaping situations. Basically, a spokeshave is a very nimble plane, with a short sole that can follow convex and concave surfaces. A good shave can follow an S-curve and leave a surface that needs little further attention.

Any time you have a part that you can't plane evenly because of its shape, there is probably a spokeshave that will help.

Think of all of the parts that you have bandsawn a curve into: a table apron, a leg for a hall table, parts for a music stand. While a template setup for a router or a sander will smooth the curves, it takes time to make the template and the setup. I recently sold my inflatable sanding drum because I could almost always spokeshave a part to smoothness more evenly and quickly. Even when I template-rout bandsawn parts, I finish them with a shave.

Start with a Metal-Bodied, Flat-Bottomed Shave

I have been using shaves to shape my chair parts for 18 years and have about a dozen or so, each with its own purpose. If you don't own a shave, you have a lot to choose from. There are flat and round-bottomed shaves, and you can buy a shave that is concave across its width, which leaves softer facets on round parts. Then there's the whole group of wooden shaves, in which the blade rests directly on the wood for the lowest possible cutting angle. But a metal-bodied, flat-bottomed spokeshave is the most versatile and gives the greatest chip control.

This standard spokeshave is inexpensive, but it requires a tune-up. The tuning process has the obvious benefit of improving the tool's performance, but it has an even more important role in developing your understanding of the tool. You'll quickly identify problems in your shaving work, and I bet you'll keep the blade sharper after you've so lovingly refined the tool.

Although there are a number of metal shaves on the market, their tune-up checklists are the same. The metal shave that shows up most often in my students' toolboxes is the Record No. 151, so for simplicity, I'll use this one as a demonstration.

I break down a major tune-up into three manageable tasks, most of which can be accomplished quickly. You don't have to go through all three steps to improve your tool; the first two will make

A Three-Step Process for a Major Improvement

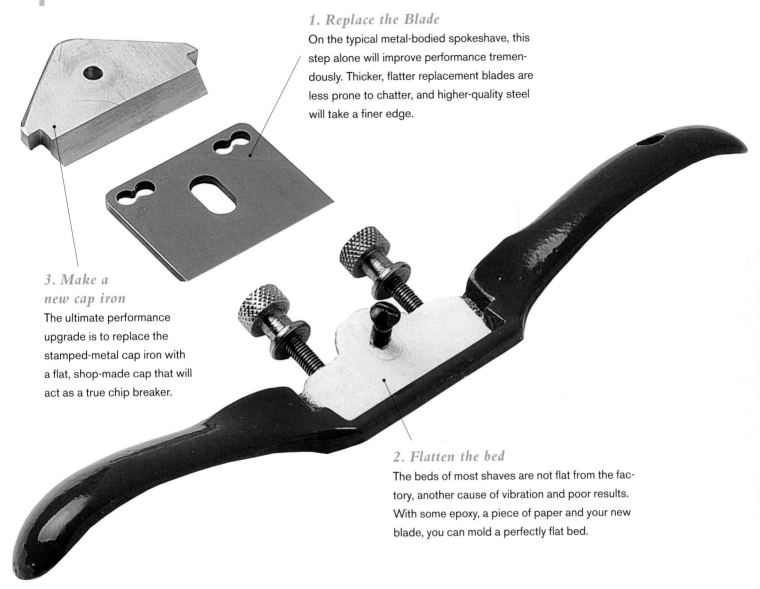

1. Replace the Blade

On the typical metal-bodied spokeshave, this step alone will improve performance tremendously. Thicker, flatter replacement blades are less prone to chatter, and higher-quality steel will take a finer edge.

3. Make a new cap iron

The ultimate performance upgrade is to replace the stamped-metal cap iron with a flat, shop-made cap that will act as a true chip breaker.

2. Flatten the bed

The beds of most shaves are not flat from the factory, another cause of vibration and poor results. With some epoxy, a piece of paper and your new blade, you can mold a perfectly flat bed.

a big difference. But once you see how much better the tool performs, I think you'll want to go all the way.

Step 1: Changing the Blade is Easy and Effective

Sharpening any edge tool is basic to getting it to work properly, but if the blade won't take an edge well or hold it for long, you are going to be frustrated.

Spare yourself some agony and purchase a good blade. Typically, the original blades are so warped that by the time you flatten both sides and get them to rest solidly in the bed, you'll wish you had bought a good blade to start with. I have used replacement blades from Hock Tools as well as from Glaser Engineering. You will get a Hock blade ($32★) more quickly, but you'll save yourself some lapping time with a Glaser blade ($28★). The latter is lapped flat with the edges finely ground and honed by hand.

Both replacement blades are available in A-2 steel, which holds an edge beautifully. In my shop tests it holds an edge six to

1. Replace the Blade

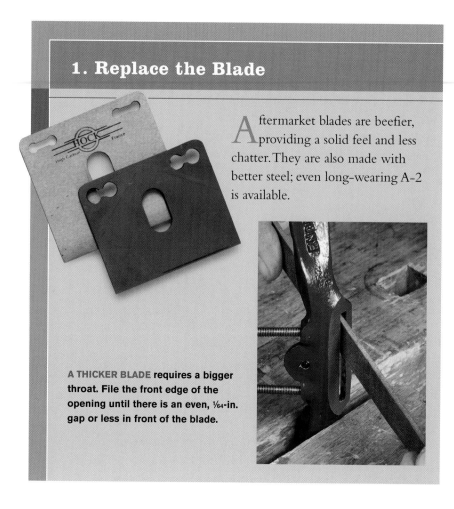

Aftermarket blades are beefier, providing a solid feel and less chatter. They are also made with better steel; even long-wearing A-2 is available.

A THICKER BLADE requires a bigger throat. File the front edge of the opening until there is an even, 1/64-in. gap or less in front of the blade.

eight times longer than regular carbon steel but takes a very fine edge almost as quickly with the same honing techniques.

You may find that the new blades are a bit thick and won't quite pass through the throat. That's okay because it forces you to open the throat by filing it, and you can true it up in the process. This opening should be less than 1/64 in. wider than the blade, just enough for a shaving to squeeze through.

Step 2: A Level Bed Eliminates Chatter

The bed, or frog, on most shaves is a painted metal surface that can be filed. But filing an area that you can't see well or hold firmly with a clamp is a fine art. I prefer to be practical here and save the art for wood-

working. I simply level the bed with epoxy, using the blade itself to mold the new bed.

This method will work for any blade, but if you start with a dead-flat replacement blade you'll make a flat bed, which then will work for any other flat blade you use. (Hopefully, you'll enjoy using your shave enough to wear out blades.)

Often the blade-adjustment screws aren't perpendicular to the bed, and the knobs, instead of turning freely in the slots in the blade, hold the blade off the bed. Also, if the holes in the knobs aren't centered, the knobs will lift the blade in some positions but not others. Find the high spot (if there is one) on the highest knob, and wrap that spot with two layers of masking tape. The tape will hold the blade clear of the adjustment knobs.

Molding a new bed in epoxy To start, apply a thin but complete coat of wax to the back of the blade as well as to the center (hold-down) screw. Allow that to dry, then buff. Now clean any oil off the bed with mineral spirits and dry carefully. Scratch the paint with heavy sandpaper or a file for a good bond with the epoxy.

Next, cut a strip of paper to go on top of the epoxy, making a better sliding surface for the blade. Also, before applying the epoxy, place two layers of masking tape over the front edge of the blade to maintain an even throat opening as you clamp down the blade onto the soft epoxy.

Whip up a batch of epoxy with a working time of 20 minutes or more, and apply an even layer to the bed. You could use auto-body filler here, too. Use just enough epoxy to fill the voids, unless you have crooked adjustment screws and need to raise the blade off the bed. For a thicker bed, wait until the epoxy firms up slightly before inserting the blade and clamping it down.

Place the paper carefully over the bed, centering the hole for the cap screw. Now

2. Flatten the Bed

A BUMPY BED and crooked adjustment screws prevent a solid connection between the blade and the tool.

THE BLADE SHOULD NOT RIDE on any part of the adjustment knob. If it does, it is being lifted off the bed of the tool.

FIND THE CULPRIT and apply a bit of tape. Before putting down epoxy and clamping the blade in place, add two layers of masking tape to the highest knob so that the blade will clear it later.

APPLY A LAYER OF EPOXY to the bed. If the masking tape and the high knob are lifting the blade off the bed considerably, add a thicker layer of epoxy and allow it to firm up slightly before clamping down the blade.

ADD A SHEET OF PAPER to provide a smooth surface for the blade. Have this strip cut to size beforehand, with a hole punched out for the center screw.

USE THE STOCK CAP IRON to clamp the blade in place. The blade will create a flat bed to support it completely. Use the center screw to apply even pressure.

REMOVE EXCESS EPOXY. Some epoxy will squeeze out around the paper, but it's easy to trim and pare cleanly.

3. Remake the Cap Iron

The underside of the stock cap iron is the problem. Because its leading edge is rounded, it has a tendency to catch shavings. So much metal would have to be removed to flatten the bottom that it simply is easier to make a new cap iron.

Rounded edge on stock cap iron.

Shopmade cap iron can act as a true chip breaker.

THE SIDE NOTCHES MUST BE FILED to the correct depth. Use a wood guide block to keep the file level. When fully seated, the cap iron should stop about 1/64 in. from the front edge of the throat.

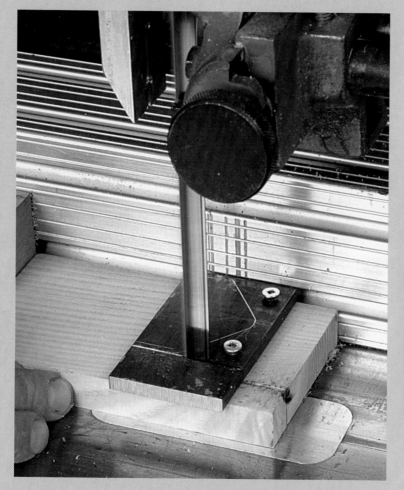

IF THE TEETH ARE FINE, a wood-cutting bandsaw blade will cut brass. Screw the brass stock to a wood scrap for safer and easier handling. Put the screws through the waste areas. Grind an even bevel along the front edge.

NEXT, MARK FOR THE CENTER HOLE. This simply is a clearance hole for the center screw, which threads into the body of the tool.

MOUNT THE CAP BACK onto the wood block for drilling. A screw clamp makes a good vise. Next, use the bandsaw to cut the corners off the back edge.

LAST, BURNISH A VERY FINE BURR on the front edge. This will create a tight seal against the blade, preventing chips from slipping underneath. Flatten the hook slightly on a bench stone.

assemble the shave, using just the center screw to hold down the blade. Use only enough screw pressure to hold things in place while the epoxy dries. Too much pressure might flex the blade and create a bowed bed. Also, if you have one high adjustment screw, be careful to lay the blade in level. Don't let it droop over the other adjustment screw. And make sure the blade is extended through the throat so that the bevel clears the bed area.

If in the first step you filed open the throat too much, use a piece of veneer or card stock instead of paper. The veneer also can be added later, glued to the paper.

Let the epoxy set up overnight. Then take apart the tool and trim the paper and any epoxy squeeze-out. Lap the bottom flat using a diamond plate or simply sandpaper glued on glass. Then file a ½-in. chamfer on the front edge of the bed and on the leading edge of the sole. Sharp edges here will scrape your wood.

Done well, these first two steps will yield a fine cutting tool that will take most straight-grained woods to a beautiful finish. You might want to stop here and enjoy some woodworking for a while, but eventually you will encounter difficult areas that don't want to shave clean no matter which direction you cut. Skewing the blade will help, but to get a perfect finish all of the time, you need perfect chip control. When you're tired of sanding almost-perfect finishes, you're ready to replace the cap iron.

Step 3: Shopmade Cap Iron Reduces Tearout

On most spokeshaves the cap iron is just a crude hold-down that keeps the blade in place. But it can do more. A flat, correctly positioned cap iron can act as a chip breaker for finer cuts with less tearout, just like the chip breaker on a smoothing plane.

The manufacturing process used on a cap iron leaves the bottom edges rounded. But without a machinist's surface grinder,

it is difficult and time-consuming to get a
stock cap iron dead-flat. I think it is far
quicker and easier simply to start over. A
quick cap iron can be made from ¼-in.-
thick brass bar stock. A steel cap is fine too,
but brass is much easier to work and can be
cut at the bandsaw with a fine-toothed
wood-cutting blade. Of course, you also can
use a hacksaw. The best place to get a scrap
of brass bar stock is a local machine shop.

You can form the back edge of your
new cap iron to the shape of the stock cap
iron, or you can just leave it long. The
important areas are the beveled chip-breaker
edge and the small ears that rest in the
notches in the body. These locate the chip-
breaker edge.

Before sawing the stock to width,
mount it on a flat scrap of wood, as shown
in the sidebar on pp. 100–101. This will
make it easier and safer to hold the stock
for sawing, grinding, and drilling. Use a
6-tpi (or finer) blade at least ⅜ in. wide, if
possible, to handle the added pressure of
cutting metal. Cut the notches only roughly
to size because you're going to do the final
fitting with a file.

Next, grind an even bevel along the
front edge. For this I clamp the stock in a
vise and pivot a belt sander on its back
edge. Check for square and make any necessary adjustments.

Check your fit and file the notches as
needed. You won't need the slotted hole the
original has; just drill a slightly oversized
clearance hole.

When the cap iron is close to the edge
of the blade and acting as a chip breaker, a
good seal is critical. To help this I burnish
the leading edge of the cap iron just as I
would a scraper, throwing a burr toward the
blade. A little lapping evens out the burr.

When you assemble the tool for use,
apply just enough screw pressure to keep
the tool from falling apart while you use it.
Tighten it only when the blade slips out of
adjustment.

You should know that even a well-tuned
shave requires practice to master. However,
with your souped-up shave, practice should
be a lot more fun.

★ Please note that price estimates are
from 2002.

BRIAN BOGGS is a chairmaker and chairmaking
instructor in Berea, Ky.

The Scraper Can Replace a Stack of Sandpaper

BY PHILIP C. LOWE

Tired of sanding? Fed up with the hours of drudgery, the clouds of dust, and the high costs? There is one simple tool that can get rid of rasp, saw, gouge, and milling marks, shearing away feathery layers at each stroke and leaving a smooth surface.

The principle behind the card scraper is simple: Take a piece of flat steel about the size of an index card. Polish an edge and rub it with a metal bar to create a sharp burr, or hook. Then flex the scraper slightly with your thumbs and push it across the workpiece at an angle that allows the burr to cut the wood.

Unfortunately, many woodworkers balk at the scraper, either giving up after one stab at sharpening and using it or not even trying at all.

But they are missing out on a dirt-cheap tool that can take the place of coarse and medium grades of sandpaper and can be cut or ground into an infinite variety of custom shapes to smooth inlay, moldings, cove cuts, and most other curved and flat surfaces. Also, where sandpaper tends to round over nearby details, scrapers cut only where you want them to.

Finally, the card scraper's width is great enough to overlap marks or undulations created by a handplane or cabinet scraper, making it the logical next step in surface preparation. In fact, the card (or hand) scraper is often mistakenly called a cabinet scraper, but the latter is a spokeshave-like tool.

Sharpening Is Not Difficult

Sharpening, or burnishing, a scraper is actually a simple process. It takes a little trial and error to create a usable burr, but you have to learn it only once, and there are a few basic keys to success. Without a squarely honed edge to start with, for example, you won't get a razor-sharp burr later.

Whether your scraper stock is square or curved, large or small, the sharpening technique is the same. The first step is done on any previously sharpened scraper but should be unnecessary for a new one. With the scraper lying flat on the bench, the

Jointing the Edge

FIRST, LEVEL THE EDGE WITH A MILL FILE. Hold the file at about a 45° angle to the direction of the cut. Take care to keep the file square to the work through the entire stroke.

THEN HONE EACH SURFACE. Start with the thin edge of the scraper, moving from a coarse stone to a fine one. Then lap the sides flat.

SCRAPERS COME IN MANY SIZES AND SHAPES. Aside from the standard card and gooseneck shapes, you can grind custom profiles to fit everything from beads to curves and use thin scrapers to wrap around curves.

burnisher is forcefully dragged back and forth to flatten the previously turned burr.

The burnisher is made of hardened steel and ideally should be free from nicks and polished to a mirror finish. Burnishers come in a few shapes and sizes. I prefer a cylindrical shape with a conical point, but I believe it's no longer available. These days I suggest the triangular style that tapers to a point.

Leveling and honing the edge The next step is to place your scraper in a vise with the edge to be sharpened parallel to the benchtop. Draw-file the edge using a mill file, directing your strokes along the length of the scraper. Hold the file at roughly a 45° angle in the horizontal plane. Give thought to filing the edge straight along its length and square to the sides.

Honing the edge follows. This achieves two things: It removes any file marks and brings the edge to a polished surface, square to its sides. Honing and polishing are done on three surfaces: the narrow edge and the two flat broad sides. I suggest starting with a coarse stone to remove file marks followed by a finer-grit stone. The finer these surfaces are polished, the sharper the edge.

Burnishing At this stage the scraper is placed back in a vise with the edge to be burnished parallel to the top of the bench. Begin by drawing the burnisher across the edge, holding the tool at a right angle to the sides. Start with light pressure and increase it with each pass. This flattens any scratch marks left on the surface, again helping to achieve a sharp edge. After four or five passes at the 90° angle, tilt the burnisher slightly for the next pass, which compresses the corner, mushrooming it out along the edge. Do this to both sides of the edge, creating two working burrs.

You might ask what the correct angle is for the burnisher while creating the burr. Think of it this way: The greater the angle of the burnisher, the more you will have to tilt the scraper to get it to cut.

Your burnishing should be firm enough to feel a distinct edge on the scraper. If the edge gets rolled over too far, it can be straightened to a better cutting angle by placing the point of the burnisher behind the burr and dragging it along the inside of the hook, bending it back to a more pleasing cutting angle. This is why I prefer a burnisher that comes to a point.

Next, flip over the scraper in the vise and level, hone, and sharpen the opposite side. At this point it's best to hold the scraper in the vise between two sticks, which prevents the newly burnished edges from being damaged.

Using a Card Scraper

The scraper can be held and moved across the wood in various ways. Typically, the scraper is flexed slightly across its length when used. This prevents the corners from digging into the surface. This bend is accomplished by pushing in the center of the tool with your thumbs and pulling with your fingers at the ends, creating an arc across the cutting edge. This is not much of a curve, just enough to lift the ends off the surface.

Tilt the scraper forward at an angle that will turn up a shaving, then push it across the work surface. You also can pull the tool. In this case, use your thumbs to pull off the ends of the tool from the surface and push the center with your fingers.

A word of caution: When a lot of scraping is done, a great deal of friction occurs, which will heat up the tool and can burn thumbs and fingers. Woodworkers employ a variety of tricks to avoid blisters. Some wrap tape around their thumbs. Others place flexible rubber refrigerator magnets on the back of the scraper. There are even holders designed to properly flex the scraper and shield your fingers from the heat buildup. But I have never had a problem using just my thumbs and fingers.

A common pitfall is focusing your efforts in one spot to remove tearout. This can lead to scraping a hollow into the surface of your panel. It may not be noticeable on bare wood but will stand out after a finish has been applied.

Some other useful applications for the scraper are removing file marks after shaping a cabriole leg, or fairing moldings once they have been mitered and attached. Straight, curved, and gooseneck scrapers can be purchased, or you can cut and grind your own custom shapes.

Sometimes I take a scraper to a sheet-metal shop and have them shear off a piece to a particular width. Then, back at the shop, I grind it to suit a particular profile. A piece of an old bandsaw blade makes a good scraper blank. A narrow scraper can be wrapped around a curved surface to smooth it.

If you're tired of buying sandpaper and fed up with holding onto a loud power sander that feels like a beehive in your hand, try the scraper. It works great when sharpened correctly, and it keeps the dust down.

PHILIP C. LOWE runs a woodworking school and makes period furniture in Beverly, Mass.

Kunz No. 112 variable-angle cabinet scraper

Cabinet Scrapers

BY MONROE ROBINSON

The dining table, 13½ ft. long and 5 ft. wide, could seat 18 people. After working on it for three months, the last thing I wanted was a flaw in the top. To smooth it—all 60-odd sq. ft. of Macassar ebony that I had painstakingly resawn—I started with a handplane.

When the ebony, still rough from the bandsaw, showed signs of tearing, I turned to a cabinet scraper. It took 16 hours, but when I was done, the top was completely flat and smooth with no chipping, gouging, or tearout. And no sandpaper.

A cabinet scraper is the ideal tool for smoothing and flattening any dense hardwood, especially if the grain is difficult and prone to tearout. Figured oak, ash, or maple and most tropical hardwoods are all good candidates for surfacing with a cabinet scraper. A belt sander may remove wood as quickly as a cabinet scraper, but a scraper is much less likely to chew through veneer into the substrate or create ugly dips in the surface. A cabinet scraper not only smooths the wood's surface but flattens it as well.

Cabinet scrapers are simply tools for holding blades at a fixed angle and depth of cut. They are pushed like Western planes, and some cabinet scrapers, like the one in the photo above, look like handplanes. Others, like the one in the

photo below, look more like large spokeshaves. All hold a blade at an acute angle to the work, so a burr on the blade cuts the wood just like a hand-held scraper. But the cabinet scraper has several advantages over a hand-held scraper. Because the cabinet scraper has a sole like a plane, the amount of blade in contact with the work is limited. As a result, the cabinet scraper takes down just the high spots and skims over any low areas.

Only a Few Models Are Still Being Made

Decades ago, there were many makers and models of cabinet scrapers. These days, I know of only four cabinet scrapers still being made—Stanley's No. 80 (widely available), the Kunz No. 12, the Kunz No. 112, and the Lie-Nielsen No. 212 (see Sources on p. 112).

Prices for new cabinet scrapers range from about $30★ for a No. 80 to $120★ for the Lie-Nielsen No. 212.

Stanley No. 80 fixed-angle cabinet scraper

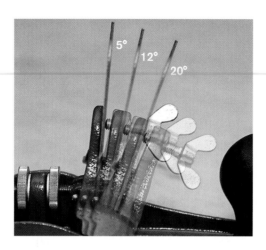

CHANGE ANGLE AS SCRAPER DULLS. The author sets a fresh blade at about 5° off vertical. When it stops cutting, he adjusts it a few degrees forward. The blade can be adjusted until it reaches 20° before it needs reburnishing.

An antique Stanley No. 112 can cost considerably more.

New or old, there are just two types of cabinet scrapers—those that hold the blade at a fixed angle and those that permit the blade angle to be set by the user. The Stanley No. 80 is a fixed-angle cabinet scraper. Both Kunz scrapers and the Lie-Nielsen No. 212 permit blade-angle adjustments. Both of these variable-angle cabinet scrapers are also called scraper planes because of their shape.

Bevel Angle Isn't Critical—A Well-Prepared Blade Is

A properly prepared blade is essential to getting a cabinet scraper to work well. All of these cabinet scrapers can be used with the blade sharpened at any angle between 90° and 45°. When filed and honed at 90° (just like a hand-held scraper), you get two cutting edges at one end of the scraper blade. A blade with a 45° angle is a more aggressive cutting tool. It will scrape for a longer period before dullness reduces it to creating dust rather than shavings. The angle is a matter of personal preference. I use a 90° angle on the blades in my No. 80s, although I know others who swear by

a 45° bevel. On my variable-angle cabinet scrapers, I prefer a bevel angle somewhere between 45° and 60°. Anything more acute than 45° would be too fragile to last very long. Whatever the angle, the bevel faces the rear of the scraper.

After filing the edge to the angle I've chosen, I hone the edge to 6,000-grit on my Japanese waterstones and burnish the edge with a light touch.

Preparing and Using a No. 80

The No. 80 is the most aggressive wood remover of the four cabinet scrapers still generally available. Because its sole is comparatively short, it's not the best tool for flattening a large surface. If not used in a consistent pattern, it can create shallow dips that would be evident when viewing the surface from a low angle, such as when sitting down at a dining table. The No. 80 is a good choice, however, for eliminating small rough spots or leveling the surface along glue joints. Or if you've already largely flattened a surface with a plane or a cabinet scraper with a longer sole but you still have some minor tearout here and there, reach for the No. 80. Just be careful not to linger in one area of the surface, or you're likely to create a depression.

To ready this type of scraper for use, start by setting the tool on a smooth, flat surface. Loosen the center thumbscrew on the back of the scraper, and slip the blade between the body of the scraper and the pressure bar until the blade bottoms out. Then, while holding down both the blade and cabinet scraper with one hand, tighten the two nuts on the front of the cabinet scraper with the other hand (see the top right photo on the facing page). This secures the blade to the scraper body and positions the blade precisely flush with the sole. Now tighten the center thumbscrew so it just barely flexes the blade (see the bottom right photo on the facing page). This pushes the center area of the blade

Fixed-Angle Scrapers

The No. 80, the most common fixed-angle scraper and the only one still being made, is the most aggressive. Its relatively short sole makes it better suited for cleaning up glue joints (below) and fairing out areas of tearout than for surfacing large tabletops. Like all other Western cabinet scrapers, the No. 80 is designed to be pushed.

Setting and Flexing the Blade

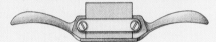

SECURE THE BLADE. Tighten the two nuts on the front of the cabinet scraper while holding the scraper body and blade down with the other hand. The blade is now flush with the sole.

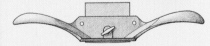

FLEX THE CUTTING EDGE OF THE BLADE. Tightening the thumbscrew on the back of the scraper body causes the blade to extend below the sole, allowing it to cut. The more the thumbscrew is tightened, the greater the blade projection.

Variable-Angle Scrapers

Variable-angle scrapers can be set again and again before the blade needs to be reburnished. The long sole on the No. 112 (below) is ideal for flattening and smoothing large surfaces, such as tabletops, especially if the wood is figured or very dense.

Adding Flex to a Variable-Angle Cabinet Scraper

By adding shims to the frog and lever, you can add flex to the end of the blade and make the cut more aggressive.

Blade

Lever shims

Frog

Lever

Frog shim

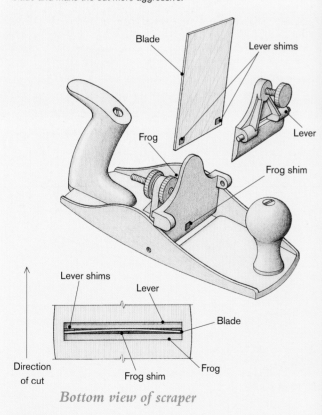

Lever shims

Lever

Blade

Frog shim

Frog

Direction of cut

Bottom view of scraper

slightly below the sole. As the blade gets dull, adding more flex with the thumbscrew will get the blade to bite again. And after reburnishing a new edge, it's often necessary to add a little more flex to get the blade to make shavings again.

Working with Variable-Angle Cabinet Scrapers

The first step in setting up a cabinet scraper with an adjustable blade angle is to position the frog mechanism to about 5° forward of straight up (see the photo on p. 108). This angle works well for a newly sharpened blade. You may want to set the angle with a protractor and bevel gauge the first time, so you know what you're shooting for. After that, setting the angle by eye is close enough. Another way is to use the cabinet scraper blade like a hand-held scraper for just a few strokes. It may feel a little awkward at first, but once the scraper's making shavings, you'll know the proper setting.

Then, just as with the No. 80, set the scraper on a smooth, flat surface, and slip the blade into the frog mechanism until it touches bottom. Tighten the blade holddown screw with one hand while holding down the blade and cabinet scraper with the other. The blade is now flush with the sole. Adjust the blade angle forward ½° or so with the blade-angle adjustment nuts at the rear of the scraper. This pushes the cutting edge of the blade back slightly so it protrudes just below the sole. The scraper is ready for use.

With use, the blade will dull. To get it to cut again, you can burnish a new cutting edge on the dull blade, adjust the angle forward or do both. The farther forward you adjust the blade, to as much as 25° or so, the more aggressive the cut. Each time I shift the blade angle forward, I reset the blade flush with the bottom. Then I shift the blade forward another ½° or so, so it's just slightly below the sole. This two-step repositioning of the blade alters the angle of the

Extended Body Gives Scraper More Sole

While attending woodworking school, I built a large, rosewood-veneered table. When I surfaced the top, I wanted to take every precaution to prevent planing or scraping through the veneer. I had an antique Stanley No. 12½, a relatively short-soled cabinet scraper, but not a No. 112, which is considerably longer. To get the longer sole I wanted, I built and attached an extended body to the old No. 12½, tripling the length of its sole and all but eliminating the chance of scraping through the veneer (see the photos above). The construction of the extended body is straightforward, all screws and glue. It works so well that it's the cabinet scraper I reach for to this day.

If you want to make your own extended-body cabinet scraper, buy a No. 12½. The No. 12½, unlike the No. 12, has four holes in the sole to fasten the extended sole to the cabinet scraper. With the No. 12, you'll have to drill and tap screw holes yourself or pay a machinist to do the work. Don't make the extended sole any thicker than 5⁄16 in. or so. If you do, the blade won't be supported very well where it scrapes and could chatter or cut poorly.

blade without causing it to protrude excessively through the bottom of the sole.

Problem-Solving for Variable-Angle Cabinet Scrapers

Much of what you've read about tuning up handplanes is just as applicable to cabinet scrapers: A flat sole and flat seating for the

Sources

MacBeath Hardwoods
510-843-4390 or
800-479-9907
www.macbeath.com
for store locations
Kunz No. 12

Lie-Nielsen Toolworks
P.O. Box 9
Warren, ME 04864
800-327-2520
www.lie-nielsen.com
Lie-Nielsen No. 212

blade will go a long way toward improving performance. But particular makes and models of cabinet scrapers seem to have some specific problems.

Every one of the dozen or so Kunz scrapers I've seen has had significant play in the pin or screws attaching the frog assembly to the scraper body, making it difficult to set the scraper iron accurately. None of the many old Stanleys I've seen have had this problem. I was able to correct the problem on a Kunz No. 112 in less than 10 minutes by flaring the ends of the screws securing the frog assembly on each side with a hammer and center punch.

Something else I noticed while experimenting with cabinet scrapers early on was that because the variable-angle cabinet scrapers don't have any provision for flexing the blade, they don't cut as aggressively as I'd like. What they needed, I figured, was a slight flex at the end of the blade, just as you would get with a hand scraper or with the No. 80. I cut three ¼-in.-sq. pieces of brass shim stock (between .020 in. and .030 in. thick is about right) and glued one on each outside corner at the bottom of the lever and one at the bottom center of the frog (see the drawing on p. 110). Wood veneer between 1/30 in. and 1/50 in. thick would work as well. Contact cement works perfectly to adhere either material to the scraper body. With these shims installed, the more you tighten the blade into the cabinet scraper, the more the blade will be flexed.

Scraping a Large Surface

Cabinet scrapers can be used to surface furniture parts of any size and, in fact, the Lie-Nielsen No. 212 works particularly well on smaller pieces. But where most cabinet scrapers really shine is on large, flat panels like tabletops.

In general, my process for flattening and smoothing a large tabletop is first to hand-plane it and then scrape it with a Stanley No. 112 or No. 12½ (same as the No. 12 but with screw holes in the sole) with an extended body (see the sidebar on p. 111). I finish up with some finer hand scraping. If the wood doesn't respond well to the handplane, I go straight to the cabinet scraper. Either way, when I do get to the cabinet scraper, I scrape the top in all directions—across the grain, diagonally in every direction, and with the grain—so I don't favor or neglect any portion of it. The order is not important, but scraping in repeated sequence from each direction is, until an overall flatness is achieved.

Once the surface has been flattened, you can use a No. 80 to remove more wood, working on small imperfections or tearouts. Or you can just continue using the No. 12 (or No. 12½) or No. 112 to do this. Although it will take longer, the top will be flatter.

The last thing I do with the cabinet scraper is hone a blade so it's very sharp, put it in my extended No. 12½ or No. 112, set it for a very delicate bite and scrape straight with the grain. I do not hold the cabinet scraper nose forward in line with the direction of the stroke. Rather, I skew the scraper first to one side and then the other. This prevents the cabinet scraper from creating a miniature washboard effect on the wood surface.

Finally, I go over the surface one last time, taking just a delicate scraping with a freshly honed hand-held scraper. The surface is now ready for a finish. And no sandpaper is needed.

★Please note price estimates are from 1997.

MONROE ROBINSON is a sawyer in Little River, Calif., specializing in the custom sawing of salvaged, old-growth redwood and Douglas fir. He was a professional furniture maker for 22 years and trained with James Krenov at the College of the Redwoods.

The Buckhorn Scraper

BY SCOTT WYNN

An odd-looking scraper caught my eye at a tool swap several years ago. It had a round wooden body with handles flared out like horns, and the sole was curved along both its length and width. The old-timers called it a buckhorn scraper. I could see it would be comfort-able to use, and that the handles would increase leverage and control. Thinking it a mere curiosity, I put the scraper down and went on to something else.

A year or so later, I built a set of eight cherry chairs with backs coopered in two directions. I needed a way to smooth the

WOODEN-BODIED BUCKHORN SCRAPERS take only a few hours to make and can be shaped to fit the curves of any project.

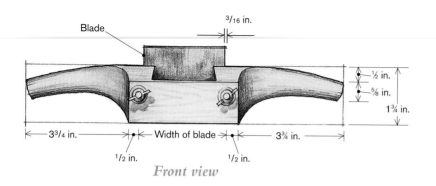
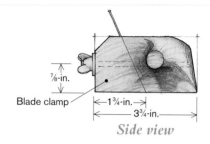

Blade

³/₁₆ in.

½ in.
⅝ in.
1¾ in.

3¾ in. ← Width of blade → 3¾ in.

½ in.
½ in.

Front view

⅞-in.

Blade clamp ← 1¾-in. →
3¾-in.

Side view

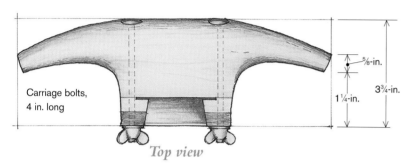

Carriage bolts,
4 in. long

⅝-in.
3¾-in.
1¼-in.

Top view

Make scraper from an 8/4 block of
dense, close-grained wood such as
maple or beech. Size it to width of blade.

1. Shape the body, and cut the blade clamp

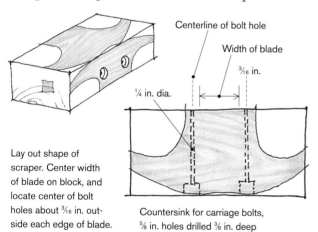

Centerline of bolt hole

Width of blade

³/₁₆ in.

¼ in. dia.

Lay out shape of
scraper. Center width
of blade on block, and
locate center of bolt
holes about ³/₁₆ in. out-
side each edge of blade.

Countersink for carriage bolts,
⅝ in. holes drilled ⅜ in. deep

2. Saw the blade clamp

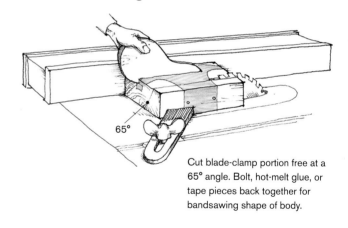

65°

Cut blade-clamp portion free at a
65° angle. Bolt, hot-melt glue, or
tape pieces back together for
bandsawing shape of body.

3. Bandsaw the excess

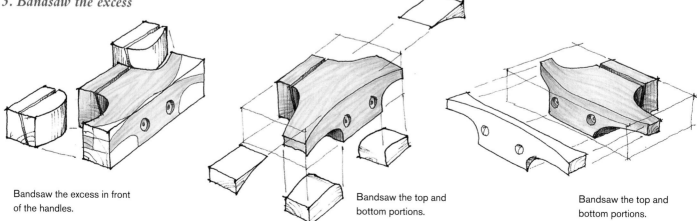

Bandsaw the excess in front
of the handles.

Bandsaw the top and
bottom portions.

Bandsaw the top and
bottom portions.

4. Cut the blade seat

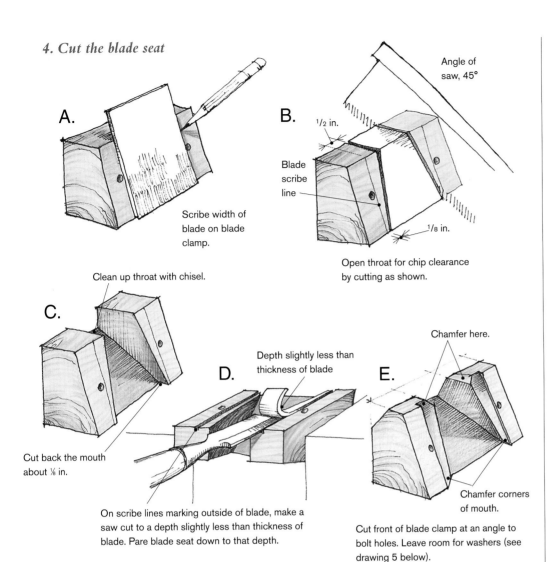

A. Scribe width of blade on blade clamp.

B. Angle of saw, 45°

1/2 in.

Blade scribe line

1/8 in.

Open throat for chip clearance by cutting as shown.

C. Clean up throat with chisel.

Cut back the mouth about 1/8 in.

D. Depth slightly less than thickness of blade

On scribe lines marking outside of blade, make a saw cut to a depth slightly less than thickness of blade. Pare blade seat down to that depth.

E. Chamfer here.

Chamfer corners of mouth.

Cut front of blade clamp at an angle to bolt holes. Leave room for washers (see drawing 5 below).

6. Shape the sole

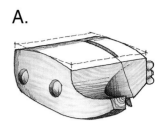

A.

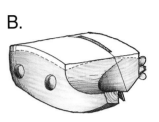

B.

Mark curves on all sides of scraper to fit workpiece. Cut or rasp curve across length of sole, as shown in drawing A. Fair curve to line. Then cut across width, as shown in drawing B. Curves in each direction should be constant. If workpiece has been roughed out fairly evenly, use it to finish shaping sole of scraper. Lay 80-grit sandpaper on work with grit side up, and rub scraper over abrasive in direction you'll be scraping. Repeat with 100- and 120-grit paper.

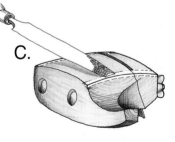

C.

Even when the sole is correctly shaped, the wood on either side of the blade may hit a high spot that lifts the scraper enough to prevent the blade from contacting the work. To avoid this, cut the sole on either side of the blade at a slightly more severe curve for the whole length of the scraper, as shown in drawing C.

5. Fit the blade seat

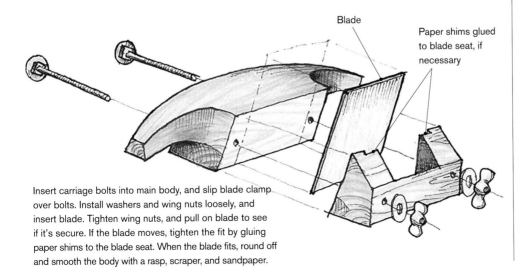

Blade

Paper shims glued to blade seat, if necessary

Insert carriage bolts into main body, and slip blade clamp over bolts. Install washers and wing nuts loosely, and insert blade. Tighten wing nuts, and pull on blade to see if it's secure. If the blade moves, tighten the fit by gluing paper shims to the blade seat. When the blade fits, round off and smooth the body with a rasp, scraper, and sandpaper.

insides and outsides of the backs, preserve their shape, and prevent grain tearout. I thought of several methods, but nothing seemed right until I remembered the buckhorn scraper. I realized that if I had a few such scrapers with the right sole configurations, I could scrape all the surfaces of the chairs smooth while maintaining the compound curves (see the photo below).

As the drawings on the preceding two pages show, I started with a block of 8/4 maple and began by shaping the flared handles. To create a blade clamp, I cut away the front of the block at an angle and bolted it in place. A little work with a handsaw and a chisel opened the throat for chip clearance. I shaped the sole to match the work and shaped the blade to the sole. In a short time, I had a comfortable finishing tool.

Shaping the Blade

I get my scraper blades from a variety of sources. I've used blades from my cabinet scrapers, bought new or used blades at tool swaps and made blades from old handsaws. A blade will often work in several other scrapers depending on the configuration of the sole. If the scrapers are curved only along their length, a straight-edged blade will work in all of them. Scrapers with the same radius curve across their width also can share blades. Because scraper blades have two useable sides, one blade can have two different profiles, further reducing the number of blades I need.

To give a blade the correct curve, I simply install it in the completed scraper so it's just barely exposed through the mouth. I mark the curve and remove the blade. When sharpened, the blade will be honed at a bevel, but when I'm shaping the blade, I grind the edge square down to the line. I check my progress frequently by reinserting the blade and sighting down the sole.

Once the blade is shaped, I grind a 45° bevel while maintaining the curve. Then I

A SCRAPER FOR ANY JOB. Over the years, the author has made a number of wooden-bodied buckhorn scrapers for concave surfaces, convex surfaces, and compound curves. Some of the scrapers can share blades.

Turning a Burr on a Beveled Scrape Blade

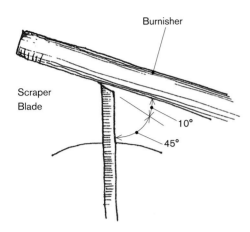

Burnisher

Scraper Blade

10°

45°

Using moderate pressure, stroke the burnisher along the bevel a few times at 45°. Then tilt up the handle of the burnisher, and take three or four strokes, tilting up the handle a little more each time. The last stroke is at about 10° to the bevel.

hone the back and the beveled edge of the scraper just as I do a plane blade. I turn the burr as shown in the drawing above.

These angles are a starting point. Harder woods often scrape best with a lesser burr angle and sometimes with no burr at all. I've also varied the bevel down to approximately 30° with good results. The hardness of the steel, the depth of the cut, the type of wood being scraped, and the curve of the sole along its length all affect the amount and the angle of the burr. Determining the optimum angles for your scrapers will take experience.

Using the Scraper

These scrapers are not tools for hogging off wood; I get the surface fairly even with a spoon-bottom or compass plane before using the scraper. If the surface isn't well-prepared, the scraper will skip, making it difficult to tell if the scraper is set properly. Initially, I set the blade in the scraper for a light cut by sighting along the sole and adjusting the blade until it protrudes evenly, just as I do on a plane. Then I make a few trial cuts.

I almost always push the scraper over the work. The difficulty in using this tool lies in keeping the blade in contact with the wood on work curved the length of the scraper. To do that, you must slightly rock the body of the scraper back and forth as you push it. Sometimes I put two fingers on the clamp portion of the scraper to get better control (see the photo on p. 113). Even so, there are strokes where the blade makes no contact.

I adjust the blade with a well-placed mallet tap and strike only the main body of the scraper, not the blade clamp. Lightly tapping the block behind the blade will back it out a little, and tapping behind the blade at one corner will angle the blade. Tapping the blade itself sets it deeper (not an option when the top of the blade also has an edge). Another way to advance the blade is by tapping the sole with a mallet.

Once I've scraped the entire surface, I resharpen the blade, back it off to a lighter cut and scrape again. I follow this with a small flexible scraper to remove any ridges. Then I sand with 120-grit paper on a shaped block and do the finish-sanding with 220- or 320-grit paper on a flexible rubber block.

SCOTT WYNN is an architect, designer, and builder of furniture in San Francisco, Calif.

Making Small Scrapers

BY WILLIAM
TANDY YOUNG

There's nothing like a thin scraper for leveling a coat of lacquer or varnish, for easing an edge, or for bringing a delicate inlay flush with its surroundings. I especially like scrapers that are small and thin. I can use them in tight corners with one hand if I have to. And small scrapers are much less likely to damage delicate details because they're easier to control than standard scrapers. Best of all, these invaluable scrapers are easy to make from pieces of good steel that find their way into my scrap-metal drawer.

Making a Scraper from a Sawblade

STEP 1

SCORE THE SAWBLADE WITH A DREMEL TOOL or die grinder fitted with a grinding wheel. The grinding wheels are available from most hardware stores. Score both sides until the piece can be bent. If you don't have a Dremel tool, an electric drill probably would work as well.

STEP 2

BEND TIP BACK AND FORTH until blade breaks off.

STEP 3

FILE OFF SCORED EDGE AND TEETH. File the edge square to the scraper's sides.

STEP 4

HONE SIDES AND EDGES. Work from your coarsest stone through a medium-grit stone. A quick, light burnishing with a piece of hard steel readies the scraper.

Sources

Garrett Wade

161 Avenue of the Americas

New York, NY 10213-0459

800-221-2942

www.garrettwade.com

I've made scrapers from old reciprocating saw blades and pieces of wide bandsaw blade, but old handsaws are one of the best sources of thin steel. When the teeth get dull on an ordinary $10★ dovetail saw, I don't bother resharpening it. It's just not worth it. Instead, I recycle the parts and buy a new saw. I tap off the handle and remove the back from the old saw. The handle gets fitted to some other tool, the back gets tossed in the scrap-metal drawer and the blade gets made into scrapers, as shown in the photos on p. 119.

Full-sized (2½ in. by 5 in. or 6 in.) thin scrapers, both rectangular and curved, are also available from Garrett Wade (see Sources). I prefer .40mm (about .015 in.) scrapers; they're half as thick as a standard Sandvik.

You can use these store-bought thin scrapers without alteration, but I usually chop them down just like the old dovetail saw. I find that thinner steel works better in smaller sizes. A thin scraper that's full size tends to flex too much during vigorous use, especially if you push rather than pull it.

★ Please note price estimates are from 1997.

WILLIAM TANDY YOUNG is a furniture maker and conservator in Stow, Mass.

Wooden Planes

BY DAVID WELTER

Making planes is one of the first things we teach in the College of the Redwoods' furniture program. These tools are essential to cabinet-making, and making one or two of them is a good way to get started. Although construction requires care, making a plane is not a difficult process, and a wooden plane is not a fussy tool to adjust or maintain. Best of all, these planes are a delight to use.

The plane body can be made of any dense, stable wood. People like the romance of an exotic hardwood; its weight feels good in use. But it can be disappointing to experiment with a precious commodity. Maple is an excellent choice for a first plane. Cherry, hickory, locust, and black walnut are other suitable common materials. Look for stock that's fairly straight-grained. A plane built from stock with tension in it will be a perpetual aggravation.

Unless the wood you've chosen for the body of the plane is especially dense and hard, you will need a tougher wood for the sole, one that is fine-textured, dense and polishes up well. Lignum vitae is the best, but it can be hard to obtain. Gonçalo alves has served our shop well for years. The

Saw a Plane Body from a Single Block of Wood

Most of the parts for a wooden plane can be roughed out from a single block of wood with just a few passes on a bandsaw. A slice of a harder and denser wood may be needed for the sole. Index pins that hold plane parts in position during assembly are cut off later.

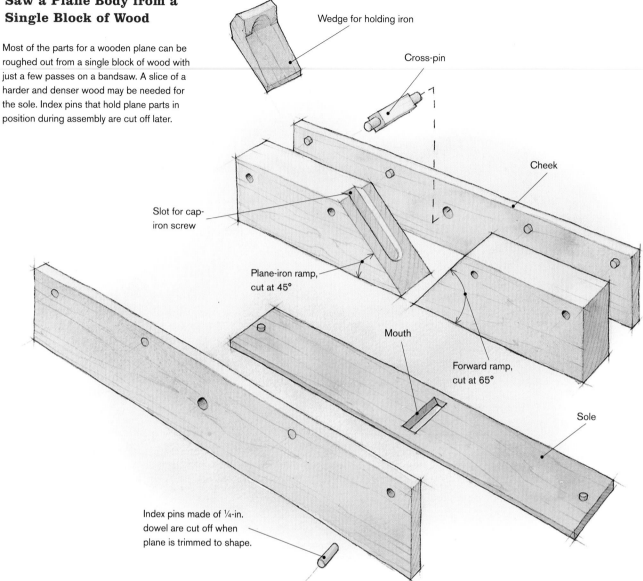

Wedge for holding iron

Cross-pin

Slot for cap-iron screw

Plane-iron ramp, cut at 45°

Cheek

Mouth

Forward ramp, cut at 65°

Sole

Index pins made of ¼-in. dowel are cut off when plane is trimmed to shape.

CUT STOCK IN THREE PIECES. Two passes on the bandsaw divide dimensioned stock into two cheeks and a center block.

DIVIDE BODY IN TWO. Cut the center block to create the halves of the plane body—a forward and a rear block.

SAVE THE WEDGE. The triangular offcut will be used later to make a wedge for the plane iron. Don't throw it out.

thickness of these dense woods should be kept to under ³⁄₁₆ in.

We use the short, thick irons made by Ron Hock for the planes we make at the school (see Sources on p. 129). You can also use a standard plane iron.

Start by Squaring Up the Block

A wooden plane starts with a block of wood that will be sliced into three sections: the body and two cheeks. There's a certain appeal to having a plane constructed from a single block of wood, but the stock also may be built up from two or more pieces. Keep balance in mind if the stock needs to be built up. The thickness of two or more joined pieces should be the same.

Minimum height for the plane blank is about 2 in. Its width is determined by the choice of plane iron, plus a finished dimension of ⁵⁄₁₆ in. for each cheek. To the width of the iron, add ¹⁄₁₆ in. to get the finished width of the center block of the plane. The extra room allows the iron to be pivoted so it's parallel to the sole without binding. Safe margins for bandsawing a solid block require 1 in. in addition to the plane iron's width; make that 1¼ in. if table sawing the block. After jointing and thicknessing the block, mark the top of the plane with a cabinetmaker's triangle to serve as a reference during assembly.

Cut the Cheeks, and Lay Out the Mouth

After cutting the cheeks on either a bandsaw or table saw (see the left photo on facing page), lightly plane the mating faces of the center block and the cheeks. Plane only enough to remove the mill marks—you want the stock faces parallel.

The location for the mouth of the plane is laid out on the center block. The mouth opening should be somewhat forward of center. The exact location is not critical. Because you most often push a plane, the

Position and Index the Plane Body

To locate the forward block correctly, start by clamping the rear block to one cheek on the bench and the forward block to the sole material. One edge of the sole should line up with the bottom edge of the forward ramp. The forward block is then shifted until the plane iron can come within ¹⁄₁₆ in. of the outside surface of the sole. Mark the cheek here.

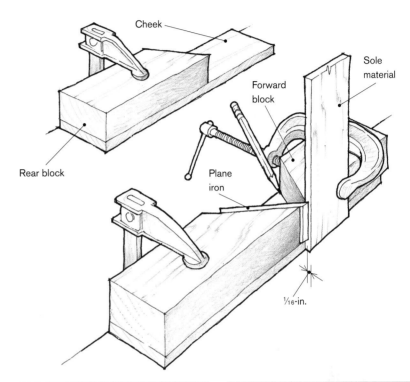

WITH BLOCKS CLAMPED, index the body. The author drills through the plane cheeks into the body to set the indexing pins.

INDEX PINS made of ¼-in. dowel hold plane parts in position during assembly. They will be cut off after the plane is finished.

back absorbs most of the effort. But a somewhat longer than usual fore section helps get the plane started correctly.

A plane-iron ramp of 45° serves well for general purpose work (see the drawing on the facing page). Exactness of that angle is less important than ensuring that the ramp is flat and square to the sides. The forward ramp, cut at about 65°, may be mildly concave to allow a little more finger room for clearing shavings. If you take this extra step, leave the lower ¼ in. at the original 65° rather than running an arc to a feather-edge at the throat opening. We cut the ramps on a bandsaw and true them up with a plane (see the center photo on p. 122). You could also use a table saw or a power miter saw. Save the cutout. It will be useful later.

Fitting Cheeks to Plane Body

To establish the positions of the forward and rear blocks, you will need the sole stock in hand. Sole stock about ¼ in. wider than the plane body will allow a margin of adjustment in alignment. Lay one of the cheeks on the bench with the inside facing

up, and place the rear block on it (the back end of the block can protrude slightly beyond the end of the cheek). Clamp the block and cheek to the bench, and draw a pencil line along the 45° ramp on the cheek.

Clamp the sole onto the bottom of the forward block, aligning one edge of the sole with the edge of the ramp (see the drawing on p. 123). Place the forward block and sole onto the cheek that's been clamped to the bench, and put the plane iron (bevel down) on its ramp. Set the iron to near cutting depth, and slide the forward block back until the sole contacts the cutting edge of the iron. Juggle the position of the blade and block until the blade touches the sole about ⅟₁₆ in. below the outside surface. Now mark the forward ramp's location on the cheek. When the plane is assembled with

Shape and Lay Out Cross-Pin

A ⁵⁄₁₆ in. hole is bored in each cheek for the cross-pin. To find the center point of the hole, lay the rear block on one cheek, and place the plane-iron assembly on the ramp. The hole is drilled at the intersection of two lines: one ⁷⁄₁₆ in. away from the plane-iron assembly and one 1¼ in. to 1½ in. up from the bottom of the block.

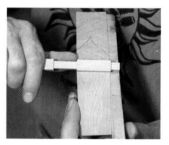

CHEEKS SHOULD NOT PINCH the cross-pin. When cut correctly, the cross-pin can rotate freely in holes bored through the cheeks.

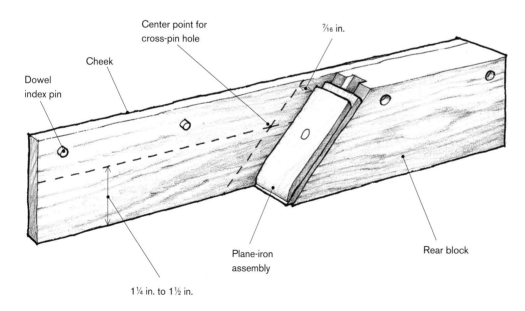

Center point for cross-pin hole

Cheek

Dowel index pin

⁷⁄₁₆ in.

Plane-iron assembly

Rear block

1¼ in. to 1½ in.

SPACING SHOULD BE EVEN. A thin strip of wood helps the author make sure the distance separating the cross-pin from the iron is uniform.

the center blocks in this position, the iron will not quite come all the way through—exact fitting will come later.

Using the lines marked on the cheek as a reference, position the center blocks between both cheeks, and clamp all three pieces together. To keep the relationship of the parts definite, index each cheek onto both center blocks with ¼-in. dowels (see the photos on p. 123). Place these index pins as near as possible to the ends or tops of the cheeks so they can be cut off when the plane is trimmed to shape.

Layout for Cross-Pin Must be Exact

Before the three pieces of the plane body can be glued together, you must cut a slot into the center of the rear block to accommodate the cap-iron screw, and you must make a cross-pin. The slot can be chopped, routed, or sawn. Cut it a little deeper than the screw head is thick, about ⅛ in. wider than the screw head, and stopped about ¾ in. from the bottom of the ramp (see the photo at right).

The center of the cross-pin falls at the intersection of two lines: one perpendicular to the bottom and the other parallel to the plane-iron ramp (see the drawing on the facing page). The pin should be high enough in the plane to allow your fingers to clear shavings from the throat and low enough for the wedge to exert pressure near the working edge of the iron.

As the drawing shows, the center point is established on the inside of one of the cheeks. That point will need to be transferred to the outside of the other cheek so that the cross-pin holes will be in line with each other. Square a line starting from the center point to the top of the cheek, across the top of the plane and then down the outside. Measure up that line, from the bottom, the same distance.

The ⁵⁄₁₆-in. holes for the cross-pin tenons can now be drilled. Drill through both

A SLOT FOR THE CAP SCREW. The rear block is slotted with a ¾-in. router bit to accommodate the cap screw on the plane-iron assembly.

cheeks from one side to guarantee that the holes will be in line (we use a horizontal boring machine, but you could use a drill press). Use the center block cutout to back up the hole while drilling to prevent blowout when the drill exits the stock. If the hole is drilled crookedly, the wedge won't grab the plane iron evenly.

First a Cross-Pin, then a Test-Fit

To make the cross-pin, dimension a 12-in. length of stock to ½ in. sq., which is more than you need. With this extra length, your hands will be well out of the way when you rough out the tenons in a crosscut sled on the table saw. And as long as the saw is set up, cut an extra pin as a backup. The length of the pin between the tenons should be slightly less than the thickness of the center block (see the top photo on

TEST-FIT. **With a cross-pin fitted in one cheek, the plane parts are brought together for a dry-fit before the author reaches for the glue bottle.**

p. 124). Once the tenons have been cut, the pin can be separated from the stock.

Trim the square tenons to fit the round holes with a knife or chisel, fairing with a file if need be. Test the size of the tenon in a hole drilled in scrap stock. The cross-pin should turn freely when in place.

All the parts are now made (see the photo above), and when you assemble them, you'll get your first look at a nearly completed plane. You still need to check that the space between the plane-iron assembly and the wedge is uniform. One way to do this is to make a tapered gauge from a thin piece of wood (the gauge also will serve as a template for making the wedge). With the plane-iron assembly in place, push the gauge between it and one end of the cross-pin (see the bottom photo on p. 124). Mark the gauge at the point where it becomes snug. Move the gauge to the other end of the cross-pin, and compare the point of snugness to the mark. Make adjustments by planing the pin, ensuring that the surface is kept straight. Note left and right on the pin if an adjustment is made.

Reach into the mouth opening to make sure there is enough finger room to clear away shavings. The cross-pin can be whittled down or the forward ramp adjusted so that the throat is accessible. Ease the corners of the pin that face away from the plane iron. Those soft corners will be easy on your fingers.

Don't Skip the Final Dry-Fit

A dry run of the glue-up greatly reduces the chance of disappointment. Make sure that neither the index pins nor the cross-pin tenons protrude beyond the cheeks (if so, they will interfere with the cauls used in glue-up). Use ¾-in. cauls the same size as the cheeks both to protect the wood and to disperse clamp pressure.

Have enough clamps on hand to be able to place them 2 in. to 3 in. apart. When the clamps are in place, be sure the cross-pin rotates. If the shoulders are tight, they might prevent the cheeks from coming home. Alignment of the center blocks can be ensured by clamping them down to a block or bench before clamps are applied to the cheeks. Once a few clamps are in place, the first ones can be removed.

I like to have newspapers and a damp rag on hand for the glue-up. Leave the cross-pin in one of the cheeks. Spread glue on the first cheek, staying about ½ in. away from the mouth opening. Position the center blocks onto the glued surface, and apply glue to the dry sides. Then place the second cheek, and start clamping. Remove any glue squeeze-out from the mouth opening with a stick and a damp rag.

The clamps may be removed after several hours, but the glue should cure at least overnight before doing further work. When the assembly has dried, the bottom of the plane may be trued with light passes on the jointer.

True Up the Plane Body with a Wedge Installed

The pressure of the wedge against the iron can cause distortion in the bottom of the plane. That condition can be taken care of in this truing process. Cut one scrap of wood that represents the plane-iron assembly in width and thickness and another for a temporary wedge. Place the faux iron in the plane, and seat the wedge firmly, but not aggressively. Resist the temptation to skip making the stand-in iron from wood. An iron that vibrates loose while jointing will most likely lead to disaster.

Care must be taken that jointing is done parallel to the bottom of the center blocks. Check as the work progresses that the throat opening appears squarely across the bottom. When the surface has been cleaned up, check the trueness on the jointer table by pushing on each corner of the plane body in turn. If the opposite corner lifts off the table, there is still an inaccuracy to deal with. If squareness of the sides is an issue,

GLUE AT LAST. **Cauls should be about the same size as the plane cheeks to ensure that clamping pressure is spread evenly. The author uses ordinary white PVA glue to bond the parts.**

Locate and Cut the Mouth

The best time to cut a mouth, or opening, for the plane iron is before the sole is attached to the body of the plane.

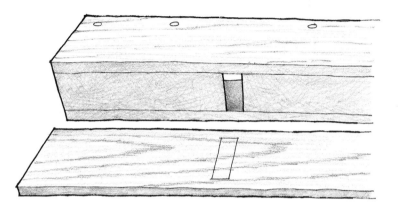

1. Lay the plane body on the sole, and mark the outline of the opening.

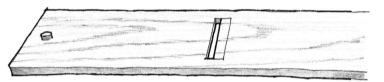

2. Cut the slot with a chisel or router, ⅛ in. wide for a standard iron and ¼ in. wide for a thick iron. Position the sole on the bottom of the plane body so the iron comes within ¹⁄₃₂ in. of the bottom surface of the sole. Ideally, the forward edge of the slot will line up with the forward ramp. Clamp and index the sole.

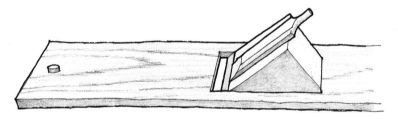

3. Take the sole off the plane, and carry the 45° angle through the sole, using the offcut of the center block as a guide. Now glue the sole to the body.

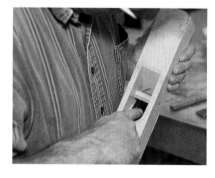

CLEANUP. **The author uses a chisel to make sure the plane iron ramp and the bevel in the slot are in line.**

SQUARE UP THE THROAT. **A file fine-tunes the throat opening. To avoid tearout, cut on the push stroke only.**

square them in reference to the bottom after it has been trued.

Adding the Sole and Wedge

The opening for the plane iron in the sole must now be laid out and cut. Before you do, though, determine which end of the sole piece should be at the front of the plane. Run your fingertips lightly from one end to the other. A sensitive touch will reveal that one direction is smoother than the other. Orient the sole so the fur runs from front to back. The drawing at left shows how the slot is laid out and cut in the sole.

When you do the glue-up, use cauls on the top and the bottom. The top caul should span the mouth opening to allow the clamps to be placed uniformly along the plane's length.

While the glue is drying, the wedge can be roughed out. Its slope is critical. It should allow for a short range of tightness. If the slope is too slight, the wedge can be driven to an excessive degree; if the slope is too great, the wedge will be either loose or tight and tend to pop out. A slope of about 1:10, or 6° to 8°, is just about right.

The offcut from the center block has enough stock to provide for the wedge. (You do still have it, don't you?) Lay it out so the grain runs along the length of the wedge. The top end should be broad enough to present a good target for tapping with a hammer and rise away from the iron so you can tap either the iron or the wedge, but not both at the same time (see the top photo on the facing page). Bandsawing is the safest way to work with such small stock. The wedge should be at least ¹⁄₁₆ in. narrower than the thickness of the center block so it can be wiggled out when you want to remove the iron.

After you've removed the clamps from the sole, make sure the bevel in the sole is truly in line with the plane-iron ramp. Any protrusion here will give a false reading

Sources

Hock Handmade Knives
16650 Mitchell Creek Drive
Fort Bragg, CA 95437
888-282-5233
www.hocktools.com

CENTER BLOCK OFFCUT becomes the wedge. The author details the plane's wedge, which should be cut to a slope of 6° to 8°. A flat at the back presents a good surface for the hammer.

when fitting the throat opening and will create a bump on the bottom of the sole. Lay a sharp chisel on the ramp, raise it slightly, and pare away excess sole material.

The remaining truing of the plane may be accomplished by lightly sanding the sole on a strip of 120-grit sandpaper clamped to a table saw (see the photo at right). Place the plane iron in the body so it nearly comes through the sole, and seat the wedge firmly. Check for inaccuracies with a straightedge both along the plane's length and across its width. The tension exerted by the wedge tends to create a bump behind the iron. With gentle pressure in the problem area, make a light pass on the sandpaper, and make sure that material is indeed being removed from where it ought to be. Don't use too much force. This task is complete when the entire surface has been uniformly abraded.

I aim for a final throat opening of about 1/16 in. Work from the outside in with a file, angling slightly toward the front to provide

EASY DOES IT. The author uses 120-grit sandpaper clamped to a flat surface to true up the sole of the plane. Using very light pressure, he sands only until the surface is uniformly abraded.

USING A NEW PLANE IS A DELIGHT. After it's adjusted with a few taps of a light hammer, the plane can get right to work. It will need very little maintenance.

shaving clearance. Remember that a file cuts only on the forward stroke. Pressure on the backstroke will likely produce chipout at the opening.

Making Your First Shavings

You are now at the point you have been anticipating: making shavings. Place the iron assembly in the body at a height above where it would begin to cut, and lightly tap in the wedge.

We have all been taught in our early years to gauge the depth of the iron by sighting along the bottom of the plane from the front. A sharp, finely set iron's edge is difficult to see in that manner. I find it much easier to adjust the iron while sighting from the back of the plane. The iron should barely present itself above the sole. It's important to get the blade parallel to the sole. If the iron is set too deeply, rap the back of the plane to back it out, set the wedge and begin again.

Two problems often show up with a new plane that can be attributed to a bump on the sole behind the iron: The plane seems to dig in at the beginning of the cut and then skate, or one of the corners of the iron constantly digs in. To correct those problems, flatten the bump with a hand scraper. It is acceptable to create a slight hollow when doing this. The plane will then sit flat when re-truing on sandpaper.

Difficulties in adjustment of the iron generally involve the wedge. Drive it in only as much as is necessary to hold the iron. A burr from the cap-iron screw may catch on the wedge. A swiveling iron may indicate that the wedge is not making uniform contact with the cross-pin. Look for burnish marks on the wedge that indicate the nature of the fit. Ease the edges of the plane, and start using it before committing to the shape of the body. An advantage to the lack of knobs and handles is that the hand's position may be shifted around in use.

DAVID WELTER has been a staff member at the College of the Redwoods in Fort Bragg, Calif., for over 18 years, and he is a contributor to *Fine Woodworking* magazine.

Wooden Chisel Plane

BY NORM POLLACK

Tools are made to fill a need. That's why the chisel plane has been around for centuries in one form or another. It's able to do some things that other planes can't do as well—or at all.

What's unique about the chisel plane is the location of the blade. It extends ever so slightly out the front, allowing a planing cut right up to an inside corner. A bench chisel can do the same thing, but the plane provides more control. The chisel plane also is useful for trimming dowel plugs flush with a surface. And many woodworkers like to use this plane to remove glue squeeze-out along a joint line.

The construction is simple enough that you can easily make one in less than half a day. It's best to make the plane from a tight-grained hardwood, like beech.

The chisel plane uses a steel blade (also called a plane iron) that's made to fit a block plane. If it's not available locally, a mail-order source for the blade and the other hardware needed can be used (see Sources on p. 134).

I like to round the heel of the plane until it fits comfortably in my hand. You may want to round it more or less, depending on what feels best for you. A shallow

THIS CLASSIC TOOL can be built in one afternoon.

A Useful Tool for a Small Investment

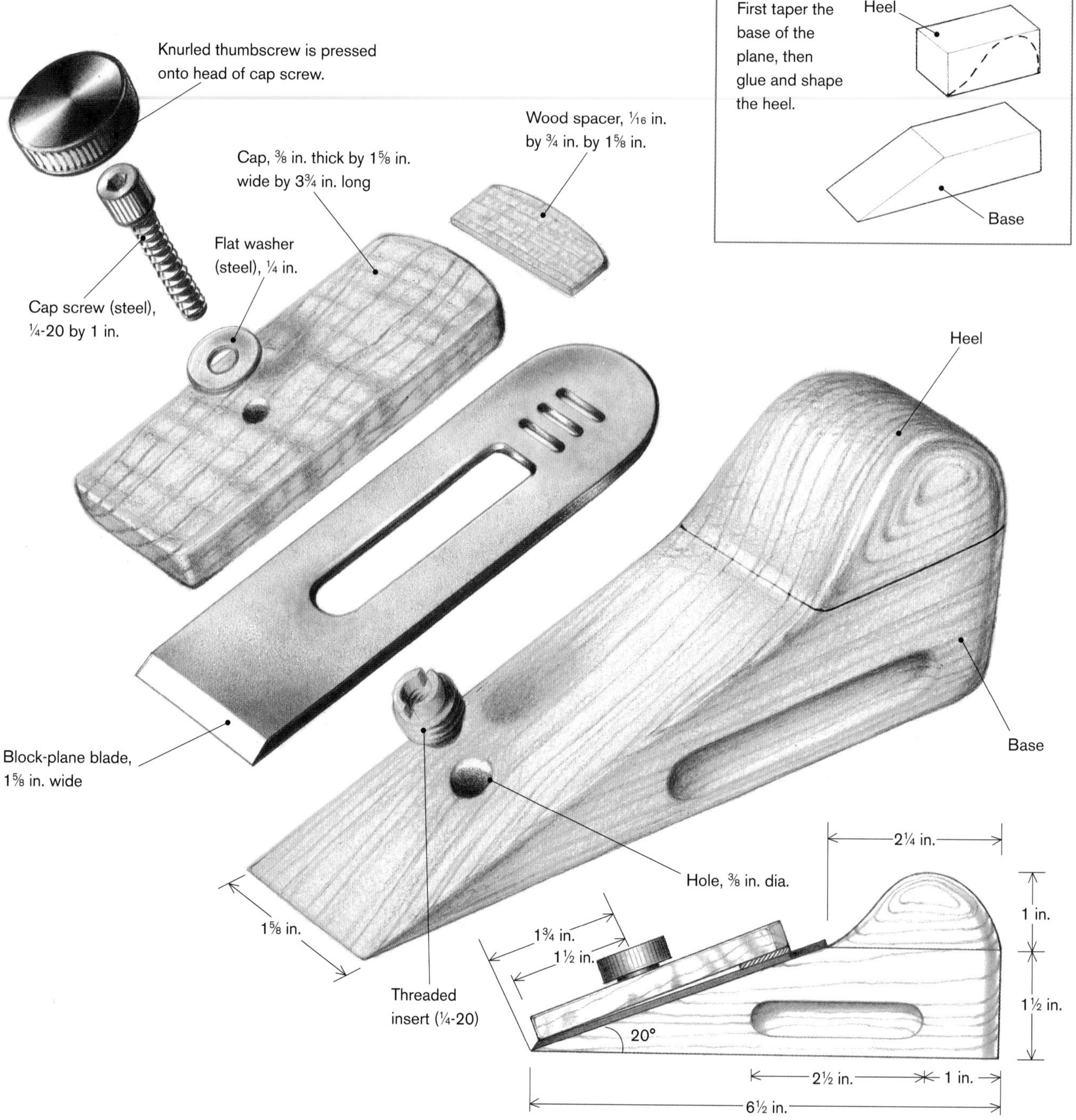

Knurled thumbscrew is pressed onto head of cap screw.
Cap screw (steel), 1/4-20 by 1 in.
Flat washer (steel), 1/4 in.
Cap, 3/8 in. thick by 1 5/8 in. wide by 3 3/4 in. long
Wood spacer, 1/16 in. by 3/4 in. by 1 5/8 in.
First taper the base of the plane, then glue and shape the heel.
Heel
Base
Heel
Base
Block-plane blade, 1 5/8 in. wide
Hole, 3/8 in. dia.
Threaded insert (1/4-20)
1 5/8 in.
2 1/4 in.
1 in.
1 1/2 in.
1 3/4 in.
1 1/2 in.
20°
2 1/2 in.
1 in.
6 1/2 in.

groove for the fingers is added, one on each side of the body, for a better grip.

Making the Body

The body of the plane has two parts—a base and a heel—which are glued together. This construction lets you cut the 20° angle of the body in a single pass on the table saw before glue-up. And because the base and heel are ripped from the same piece of stock, the glueline hardly shows once the two parts have been attached.

Start with a piece of 1⅝-in.-thick stock, measuring at least 3 in. wide and 10 in. long. Although the length here is almost double that of the finished plane, the extra material allows for some trimming that's done later. By the way, you can make two of these planes almost as fast as you can make one. If you want two planes, start with a 24-in. length of stock.

Rip the board to 1½ in. for the base. Then relocate the fence and rip the 1-in.-tall heel.

Cut the taper using a trimming jig

Now you can cut the 20° taper on the top edge of the base. This cut needs to be flat and square to the sides of the base. So to get a good cut, I made a jig that allowed me to use my table saw.

The jig is a piece of ¾-in.-thick medium-density fiberboard (MDF) or plywood, with a notch for the base (see the photo at right). Cut the jig to size and mark the location of the notch, then bore a clearance hole at the corner to prevent dust buildup. Then cut out the notch with a bandsaw, staying slightly on the waste side of the line as you cut. Sand the sawn edge exactly to the line.

Next, bore a hole in the base to accept a 2½-in. screw, which secures the base to the jig. That's important, because you don't want your hands near the blade here. Drill the hole about ⅝ in. from the end of the base and ⅜ in. from the side. If you're concerned about ending up with a plane that has a hole in it, don't worry. The end with the hole gets cut off after the taper has been cut.

Now, place the base into the jig and drive the screw. Position the rip fence so that the inside tooth of the blade is about ½ in. from the edge of the jig. Then use a long pusher to push the jig through the blade.

With the taper cut, the glue-up can start. First, though, trim the end of the base so that you end up with a 2¼-in. flat along the top edge. Then cut the heel to the same length and glue it to the base.

Rout the finger grooves

I cut the finger grooves on the router table with a ½-in.-dia. cove bit. Because each groove is hidden as you cut, you need guide lines on the body of the plane and on the fence.

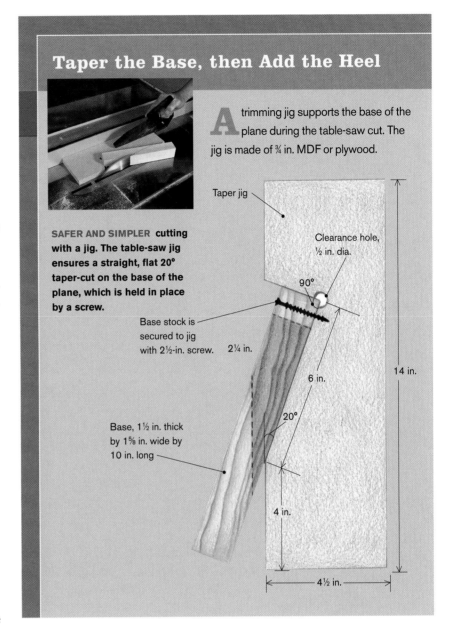

Taper the Base, then Add the Heel

A trimming jig supports the base of the plane during the table-saw cut. The jig is made of ¾ in. MDF or plywood.

SAFER AND SIMPLER cutting with a jig. The table-saw jig ensures a straight, flat 20° taper-cut on the base of the plane, which is held in place by a screw.

Taper jig

Clearance hole, ½ in. dia.

90°

Base stock is secured to jig with 2½-in. screw.

2¼ in.

6 in.

14 in.

20°

Base, 1½ in. thick by 1⅝ in. wide by 10 in. long

4 in.

4½ in.

On one side of the body, mark lines to show where the groove begins and ends. Then extend the lines to the bottom edge, where the body meets the fence. Next, with the bit installed, butt the fence against the bit and make two marks on the fence, one aligning with the left edge of the bit and one with the right edge. Use a square to lengthen both of the lines so they can be seen when the body of the plane is against the fence. To complete the setup, position the bit to extend ⅛ in. above the table, and locate the fence ¼ in. from the bit.

Now fire up the router. With the back end of the plane body on the table and the

Glue Up and Shape the Plane Body

GLUE THE HEEL onto the base. The grain at the joint line matches nearly perfectly because the two parts are ripped from the same piece of stock.

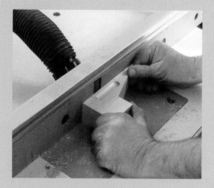

ROUT THE FINGER GROOVE. A shallow finger groove on each side of the plane is cut on the router table using a cove bit.

HAND-SHAPE THE HEEL. After band-sawing the rough shape, a few minutes with a rasp and file complete the rounding of the heel. Smooth out the file marks with sandpaper.

Sources

Reid Tool Supply Company
2265 Black Creek Road
Muskegon, MI 49444
800-253-0421
www.reidtool.com
Hardware

Woodcraft
P.O. Box 1686
Parkersburg, WV
26102-1686
800-225-1153
www.woodcraft.com
Stanley block-plane blade

bottom of the plane against the fence, lower the body into the bit by pivoting the front end down onto the table. When the body is on the table, push it to the right until the left lines on the body and fence line up. Then push the body to the left until two right lines align. Repeat on the other side.

Shape the heel in three steps First, after drawing the curve, cut the heel to rough shape with the bandsaw. Then fair the curve with rasps and files. And finally, sand the heel smooth.

Mount the threaded insert The plane's cap is held in place with a knurled, plastic thumbscrew that fits a threaded insert in the tapered face of the body.

The ¼-20 insert fits into a ⅜-in.-dia. through-hole. So you'll want to start the procedure by marking the center point of the hole on the taper.

Because the hole must be bored square to the tapered face, you'll have to tilt the drill-press table to match the 20° angle of the taper. Or, if you have a drill-press vise, as I do, you can clamp the body into the vise and use a square to make sure the taper

is 90° to the bit. Once everything is square, drill the hole.

A threaded insert has a slot that allows you to install it with a wide-bladed screwdriver. But it takes a fair amount of torque to turn the insert, so the slot quickly gets chewed up, making it harder to turn, and sometimes goes in crooked. To make this job easier I put a couple of nuts on a short length of threaded rod. One end of the rod chucks into the drill press. On the other end, the nuts butt together, allowing about ⅜ in. of the rod to be exposed.

After threading the insert up to the first nut, raise the table just enough to start the end of the insert into the hole. Then use a wrench to turn the upper nut, which turns the insert. At the same time, lower the quill to feed the insert into the wood. Don't thread the insert all the way in. Instead, I like to leave about 1/16 in. extending above the surface to help center the blade slot when it's added later.

The process of turning and feeding gets the insert installed in no time with little effort. And it's always square. By the way, to prevent the entire plane from turning as you use the wrench, clamp a stop block to the table.

Making the Cap and Adding a Finish

You'll need ⅜-in.-thick stock for the cap. After the stock has been cut to size, lay out and mark the center point for the hole that accepts the thumbscrew.

To concentrate more pressure along the front of the blade, add a thin wood spacer along the back of the cap. The added pressure in front helps keep the cap from twisting and prevents chattering of the blade. After the spacer has been glued in place, the back end of the cap and the spacer are sanded to an arch shape on a disc sander.

A penetrating oil makes a good finish for the plane. Once the finish dries, slip the slot of the blade over the end of the threaded insert. Make sure the bevel faces up. Then add the cap and snug it down with the thumbscrew and washer.

Adjusting and Using the Plane

Adjusting the blade is pretty straightforward. Loosen the thumbscrew just enough to allow the blade to move. Then, with the bottom of the plane on a flat, wooden surface, slide the blade forward. When the entire front edge of the blade just touches the wood, tighten the thumbscrew.

Because there's no support in front of the blade, a chisel plane can dig into the wood if you apply too much pressure at the front. The secret is to apply slightly more pressure at the heel.

NORM POLLACK, a retired electronic technician, lives in Woodbridge, Va., where he spends a lot of time making wooden planes.

Drill and Install the Threaded Insert

BORE THE HOLE for the threaded insert. The hole is drilled at a right angle to the tapered portion of the base. Use a vise and square to position the stock for drilling.

INSTALL THE INSERT. With the drill turned off, and with the help of a couple nuts, a threaded rod, and a wrench, the insert goes in easier and straighter.

Simple Tools Can Reproduce Most Moldings

BY ROBERT S. JUDD

Scratch stocks function beautifully, quickly, and economically to duplicate handworked wood trim. By simply grinding or filing a cutter to the appropriate profile, you can reproduce almost any shape molding up to about 1 in. wide. Scratch stocks, or beading tools as they are sometimes called, are readily available new (see Sources on p. 138), used (antique tool dealers, garage sales, or flea markets), or shopmade (see the photo below). I make mine from a 6-in.-long, L-shaped piece of stock. The cutter fits into a sawkerf, and it is clamped in place with a few screws, as shown in the photo below. The cutters for all of these tools are easily shaped from old scrapers and sawblades or new blanks from Lie-Nielsen or Veritas.

In my repair and restoration business, I often need to duplicate broken or missing

SCRATCH STOCKS. **Whether old like the Stanley No. 66 (far right), new like the Lie-Nielsen No. 66 reproduction (left) or shopmade (top), these scratch stocks are a simple way to reproduce moldings or create new designs accurately and economically.**

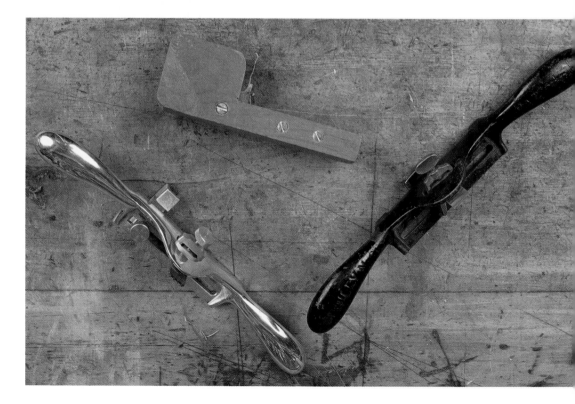

moldings. Usually, only a foot or two of the molding is needed: hardly worth the effort of setting up the router and definitely not worth having a cutter ground to match one of the myriad of molding shapes. Besides, no power tool can match the irregularities of the handworked wood found in older pieces.

Scratch Stocks and Beaders

First made by users as a simple holder for a scraper blade, scratch stocks included a fence arrangement to work a measured distance from an edge. The beading tool was essentially an improved, factory-made scratch stock and included a range of cutters in different sizes and several blanks, custom-filed to fit the user's needs. Adjustable fences for both straight and curved edges were often included. A scratch stock or beader can produce a carbon copy of the original molding by using a cutter that's simply filed to shape.

Shaping the Cutter

To make a basic beaded molding, take a sample piece of beading, a file, and a blade blank and set to work filing a negative pattern of the molding, as shown in the top left photo. As you file the pattern into the blade, keep testing its fit (see the photo on p. 138). Check the fit frequently because it is fairly easy to file past the desired shape. It's a good idea to leave a ⅛-in.-wide metal strip at either edge of the cutter. Narrower strips tend to bend and lose their effectiveness. Old cabinet scrapers or sawblade sections make good cutters for shopmade scratch stocks. But for my 100-year-old Stanley No. 66 hand beader, the blanks that Lie-Nielsen makes for his gem-like bronze replicas of the No. 66 work well. The steel of the new blanks is not hardened, so the blanks are easy to file to shape. After filing them to shape, hone just the cutter's faces in a whetstone to provide a clean cutting

FILING A CUTTER TO SHAPE. Almost any profile, up to 1 in. wide, can be filed into blade blanks made from old cabinet scrapers, sawblades, or new blank stock (above).

BEADING IS SIMPLE WITH A SCRATCH STOCK. Just hold the fence against the stock and make repeated passes, about ¹⁄₁₆ in. per pass, until the appropriate depth has been reached.

edge. I've never found it necessary to harden a cutter once it's filed to shape.

Making Moldings

When producing short moldings, I've found it easier to work the edge of my board, as shown in the bottom photo above. For making small beads or moldings, I cut two lengths at once by working both corners of the same board edge. Begin the

MATCHING A MOLDING TO A CUTTER is crucial to reproducing old moldings. File the cutter to the negative image of the molding. Check the cutter frequently while filing to make sure it is an accurate match.

Sources

Lie-Nielsen Toolworks, Inc.
P.O. Box 9
Warren, ME 04864
800-327-2520
www.lie-nielsen.com

Lee Valley Tools, Inc.
12 East River Street
Ogdensburg, NY 13669
800-667-2986
www.leevalley.com

One of the handy features of the No. 66 or the Lie-Nielsen reproduction is the adjustable fence. When cutting two lengths of molding on a board edge, the fence can be set to cut the opposite corner without moving the blade. This lets you produce a surprising amount of molding in a relatively short time. I make several extra moldings, so I can pick the best match to the original.

I like to start the staining and coloring process at this stage because the strips are far easier to handle while they are still attached to a board. Often, I will even do the preliminary finishing and filling at this point for the same reason. It's then a simple matter to trim the finished molding off on the tablesaw. I set the saw fence to leave a little extra material, which I later trim off with a utility knife.

When repairing antique pieces, mark your name and date on the back of the new molding for historical reference. After all, with a matching stain and finish, the repair should be almost invisible.

Other Applications

In addition to producing molding patterns, this highly functional family of tools is also effective for routing and inlay work. Because you create the cutters to fit the situation at hand, you are no longer limited to standard router bits.

When using these tools to rout cross-grain, however, it's a good idea to lay out the material to be removed by lightly cutting in the lines with a sharp craft knife. The scored lines help prevent tearout, which could ruin your project.

ROBERT S. JUDD is a professional furniture repairer and refinisher in Canton, Mass.

scraping process by firmly gripping the handles, and push or pull the tool across the board's edge, keeping the handles at 90° to the work. Take small scrapings initially, only $\frac{1}{16}$ in. or so at a time. Because stock removal is done by scraping, a small cut gives much more control and does less damage if you slip. As the cutter starts to bottom out, you can continuously adjust the blade so more is exposed. In a surprisingly short time, the molding will start to appear on the edge. If the cutter starts to chatter or jump, you are probably trying to remove too much material, or the grain might be changing; use a little less pressure, or try changing the direction of cut.

Scratch Stocks

THEY DON'T HAVE TO BE PRETTY. **These are some of the scratch stocks Millard has made using scraps of wood for the handles and bandsaw blades or old scrapers for the cutting blanks.**

BY ROB MILLARD

The scratch stock is a simple tool with an impressive ability to dress up furniture with distinctive decorative elements that are exactly the right shape and size. I made my first scratch stock years ago from a piece of oak scrap, and I've made a number of others since then. My shopmade tools aren't as fancy as some commercially available beading tools,

but they work, which is all that I require of them.

With scratch stocks, you can shape a wide range of moldings in both straight and curved work. The tool does have some limitations, though. Being slow, a scratch stock is not the right tool for a large run of molding. Also, it's hard to start or stop a

Beads

Flutes and Reeds

Wide Moldings

scratch stock in the middle of a board (leaving you with some handwork); nor does it work as well across the grain or on softwoods. A scratch stock is best suited for smaller shapes, but with a closely matched handle you can create some fairly wide moldings. Another approach is to use several different cutters, in stages, to obtain a surprisingly complex molding.

Start with a Basic Scratch Stock for Beads

The simplest scratch stock I make is an L-shaped piece of oak with a bandsaw kerf cut into it and two screws for clamping the cutter in place. I chamfer the guide edges of the handle to facilitate using it on concave curves with a tight radius. I make the

A Basic Scratch Stock for Beading

An L-shaped body works well to make simple beads. The cutter is placed right into the corner, where the two wood edges stabilize the blade for a clean, consistent cut. The long edge is chamfered, so the cutter can be tilted to start the shaping.

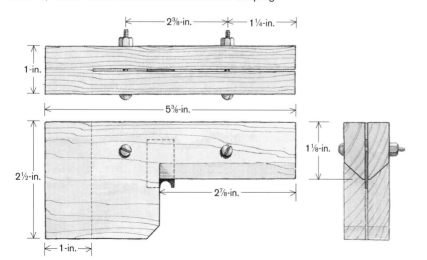

NARROW BANDSAW KERF is just right. Split the body of the scratch stock down the middle but stop the cut 1 in. shy of the end. The cutters are pinched in the kerf and held in place with two machine screws and nuts.

cutters from old cabinet-scraper blades or used bandsaw blades. I first apply layout fluid (the metal dye that some people call bluing) to the cutter blank. I use a machinist's carbide-tipped scriber to draw the profile and then begin filing to those lines using coarse files. Don't allow too much of the cutter to protrude above the vise; otherwise, it will flex, causing the file to screech and dull quickly. I finish with fine files, being careful to maintain a square cutting edge.

You can put a slight bevel on your cutter to improve the cutting action. But the bevel limits you to using it in only one direction, taking away one great advantage of the scratch stock—its ability to handle reversing grain. I also hone the faces to remove burrs. For this I use a fine, pocket-size diamond stone. I usually end up having more than one profile on a cutter, and I always keep them for future use. When laying out the cutter profile, the more the blade is supported by the handle, the better the cutter will work.

Scratch Stocks for a Variety of Shapes

Using a scratch stock couldn't be simpler: Apply light downward pressure as you firmly push the scratch stock forward or draw it toward you. At first, it helps to tilt the tool slightly in the direction of the cut, but you should make the last pass with it as close to vertical as possible to ensure a uniform profile. When possible, the cutter should be installed so that the handle will act as a stop when the full profile has been reached. Once the cutter starts to dull, it will produce dust as opposed to fine shavings. At that point you'll have to file the edge lightly and hone the face again. If I'm making more than one length of molding, I typically go over each piece one last time with a freshly sharpened cutter. Following that procedure keeps the profiles consistent.

Making a Scratch-Stock Cutter

You can make cutters using scrap metal from card scrapers and old bandsaw or hacksaw blades.

STEP 1
ADD SOME COLOR TO THE STEEL CUTTING BLANK. **Layout fluid (also called bluing) makes it easier to see scratch marks that define the shape of the cutting edge.**

STEP 2
DRAFTING TEMPLATES COME IN HANDY. **Scribe shapes on the cutting blanks using a machinist's scriber.**

STEP 3
START WITH COARSE FILES. **Remove metal waste quickly with a coarse file, then improve the cutting edge with a finer tool.**

STEP 4
HONE THE BLANK TO REMOVE ANY BURRS. **A pocket-size diamond stone is ideal for sharpening small cutting blanks.**

Because I make period furniture, I often have to reproduce moldings that don't correspond to profiles available in shaper or router bits, or that I don't have an appropriate molding plane for. I remove the bulk of the waste from a given profile using a router, then refine the profile with a scratch stock. For me, this has the added benefit of giving a handmade look to the molding.

With extremely careful use, the scratch stock can produce moldings that rival those made by machine, and in some cases surpass them, because a steel scratch-stock cutter can be filed to a much finer point than carbide tools. Also, the variety of shapes that you can make is virtually limitless.

Applied cock beads For making applied cock beads, I use two different methods. One is to work the bead on a piece of wide stock and rip it off, and the other is to clamp the scratch stock in a vise and pull a piece of material already cut to thickness over the cutter. This second method is also the one I use for cock beads that are applied to curved work. Here again, you must be careful of the cutting direction to avoid tearout.

Reeds My favorite use for the scratch stock is to cut reeds in turned Sheraton legs (see the sidebar on the facing page). This makes quick work of reeded legs, as long as the profile of the leg is a gentle taper. (A more bulbous turning requires carving the reeds by hand with a chisel because of the dramatic change in its radius.) I made a wood fixture from plywood and lumber scraps that I clamp to the bed of my lathe. The fixture acts as a guide for a scratch stock to keep it running down the centerline of the leg and more or less parallel to the taper of the leg. By using the indexing feature of the lathe, I can quickly shape the required number of 12 reeds. The ends of each reed still need to be carved by hand, and the profiles refined with chisels and a scraper.

Two Options for Applied Beads

MOVE THE SCRATCH STOCK against the workpiece. Make the cut in multiple passes, with light downward pressure as you go. On the final few passes, hold the blade as vertically as possible. Rip the bead from the stock.

MOVE THE WORKPIECE against the cutter. With the scratch stock clamped in a vise, make multiple passes. This method works well for delicate workpieces, such as cock beads that will be applied to curved surfaces.

Scratch Stock for Reeds and Flutes

Millard reeds a leg by mounting an open-ended, three-sided box on the lathe bed. The handle of his scratch-stock beading tool fits within the box and rides along the top edge of the open end. This setup allows him to control the cut better and make reeds that run straight along their length.

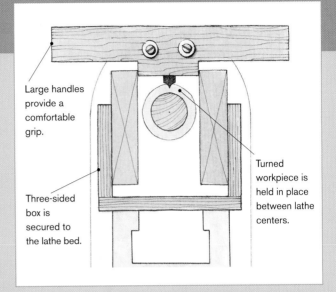

Large handles provide a comfortable grip.

Three-sided box is secured to the lathe bed.

Turned workpiece is held in place between lathe centers.

SOME ADDITIONAL HANDWORK is often necessary. Transitional areas, such as where these reeds start and stop at the top and bottom of the legs, often require additional shaping with chisels and scrapers.

Wide Moldings

Scratch stocks work best when removing only small amounts of wood. For larger or more complex moldings (such as the cove shown here), Millard often uses molding planes or small routers first, following with an appropriately shaped scratch-stock cutter to scrape the surface clean.

Flutes and Coves Fluted columns can be made with the same setup, but the process requires more care because more of the cutter protrudes from the handle, as it also does on large coves, which causes the tool to chatter. If the flutes don't run all the way through the tops and bottoms of columns, you are left with a considerable amount of hand-carving to do. But for period furniture the result is still visually superior to router-cut flutes and coves. With a scratch

stock, you're limited to fairly small cuts (¼ in. or ⁵⁄₁₆ in.) because of the flexing of the cutter, unless you construct a shaped handle that provides more support.

Curved work For use on curved work, I install the cutter in the scratch stock so that I use the short side of the handle as the driver, to lessen the tendency to rotate the tool too much when turning around a curve. With curved work, the grain changes directions continuously, so you'll have to pay close attention to the direction in which you push the cutter so that you get the best finished surface. And even then, at the areas where the direction changes, you will probably need to refine the shape of the scratch cut with carving tools.

Complex moldings With a properly made handle, you can work a molding up to at least 1½ in. wide, after removing much of the waste with a series of rabbets using a router, a shaper, or a dado set on the table saw. The handle should at least roughly follow the shape of the molding profile, leaving about ⅛ in. to ¹⁄₁₆ in. of the cutter exposed. You also can make the profile in stages—much as you would work a complex molding with a series of router bits. The limitation here is that you must have two edges that you can use to guide the scratch stock accurately.

ROB MILLARD builds one-of-a-kind reproduction furniture in his garage shop in Dayton, Ohio.

Make a Wooden Scraper

BY STEPHEN SHEPHERD

Scrapers are among the most useful of all the hand tools in a wood-worker's arsenal. Properly sharp-ened and burnished, a scraper will remove a fine shaving on even the gnarliest wood, leaving the surface with a depth and sheen that you can't achieve with sandpaper. When viewed under magnification, a scraped surface appears crisp, and the pores are clean and free of debris.

Cabinet scrapers offer advantages over the familiar, flat-metal hand scrapers (also called card scrapers). As with a handplane, the fixed relationship of the blade to the sole produces a uniform depth of cut, which you can vary by deflecting the blade with a thumbscrew. The sole also bridges low spots rather than following the contours of the surface as a hand scraper does. Last, the cabinet scraper's outswept handles provide more leverage for aggres-sive cuts while insulating the user from the heat produced by the scraping action.

All cabinet scrapers vibrate and chatter when the cut is too aggressive or the blade is dull, but metal-bodied cabinet scrapers chatter more because the metal surfaces have no dampening effect on vibration. A shopmade wooden cabinet scraper, on the

A CUT ABOVE. A wooden cabinet scraper is superior to its metal cousin for its ability to handle figured boards.

Three Views of a Wooden Scraper

These illustrations show a 3-in.-wide blade. Scale the width of your design to reflect the actual width of the blade you use.

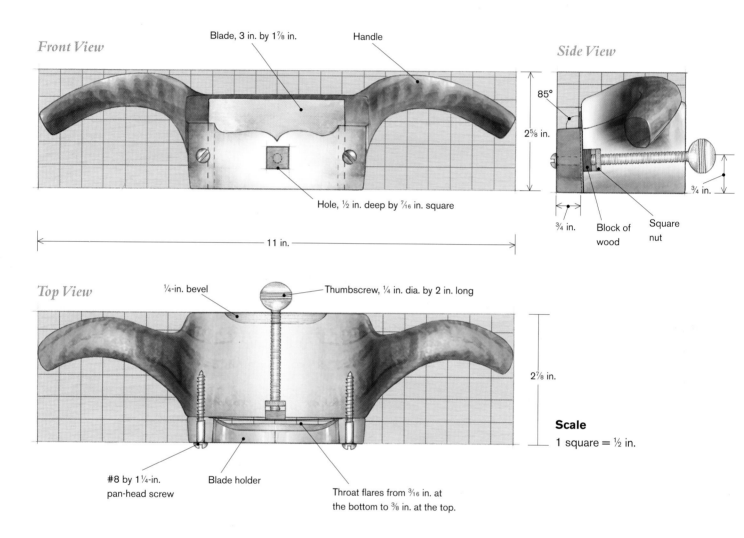

Front View

Blade, 3 in. by 1⅞ in.

Handle

Side View

85°

2⅝ in.

¾ in.

Hole, ½ in. deep by ⁷⁄₁₆ in. square

¾ in.

Block of wood

Square nut

11 in.

Top View

¼-in. bevel

Thumbscrew, ¼ in. dia. by 2 in. long

2⅞ in.

Scale

1 square = ½ in.

#8 by 1¼-in. pan-head screw

Blade holder

Throat flares from ³⁄₁₆ in. at the bottom to ⅜ in. at the top.

Sources

Woodcraft
P.O. Box 1686
Parkersburg, WV 26102
800-225-1153
www.woodcraft.com
Sandvik scraper

other hand, chatters less, is more sensitive to the wood surface, and can be customized for applications such as smoothing chair seats and rungs.

Three Main Parts Form the Scraper

Before preparing the wood for the scraper, determine the width of the blade. You can buy replacement blades for the Stanley or Kunz metal scrapers that are 2¾ in. wide. For this scraper, I used a 1¾-in.-long section

from the end of a 2½-in.-wide Sandvik hand scraper. Cut the scraper with a hacksaw or tin snips, then file the edge smooth.

Shape the body first This design is modeled after an early 19th-century example. The body of the cabinet scraper is made of a hard, smooth-wearing wood such as maple or beech, although historic examples include walnut burl, rosewood, and ebony.

Start with a piece of wood about 2½ in. wide by 3 in. high and 8 in. longer than the width of your blade. Smooth one wide face